SQL [6 BOOKS in 1]

The Ultimate Beginner to Advanced Guide to Master SQL Quickly with Step-by-Step Practical Examples | Includes Interview Questions & Answers

Liam DeSantis

Contents

Book 1: SQL For Beginners

Chapter 1: Introduction to The Language of Databases: SQL

Currently, the SQL language is accepted by most databases, and it provides a simple and intuitive way to read, introduce or modify the information contained in the tables. Knowing it is essential since practically all applications have a data repository that must be accessed at one time or another through an SQL query. Throughout this book, the basic concepts of this language will be introduced through a series of simple examples.

You could say that the SQL language provides a means of formally representing statements like, for example, "I want all the first and last names in the 'Contacts' table in alphabetical order"; or "Deletes all records from the 'Contacts' table whose phone number is blank."The goal of the SQL language is to synthesize this natural way of expressing actions that refer to tables in a database.

```
SELECT NAME, LAST NAME
FROM CONTACTS
ORDER BY NAME, LAST NAME;


DELETE CONTACTS
WHERE TLFN = '';
```

The previous examples show how the SQL language uses an intuitive syntax to faithfully capture the meaning of the everyday phrases to which they correspond.

Databases need to provide a means for users to insert, modify or query information. SQL has become a standard that is accepted by most. Although it is also true that there are considerable differences between the versions that interpret some databases and others.SQL, statements allow you to relate all the tables that make up a database, either to obtain a specific data set ordered within a particular way or, for example, to determine the collection of elements that must be eliminated. In addition, its syntax provides the necessary means to create, modify or delete tables and other aspects of databases, such as sequences, indexes, views, etc.

One of the best ways to learn the SQL language is to create a database with Microsoft Access and practice different queries. Although Access is not a complete example, and its features are not comparable to those of other large databases, its ease of use and diffusion makes this application a perfect choice.

Creating a database

With Access, creating a database is very easy. The following points show the steps to follow:

Step 1: New Database

Double-clicking on the program icon opens Access. A window is automatically displayed that offers the user three possibilities. Among all of them, you must select "Blank Access Database."

Step 2: .mdb

File Access databases use .mdb files to store information. The next step is to select the directory on which you want to save the file and its name.

Step 3: Main Database

Window The main window contains most of the options and menus you will use during a typical Access session. To create a new table, select the option "Create a table in Design view."

Step 4: Define the name and type of the fields

In the left column, you must enter the name of the fields and their type in the right column. This can be chosen from a list that appears automatically when typing or clicking the mouse. In the lower area of the screen, there is also a tab that allows you to configure parameters such as the mandatory nature of a field or, for example, the maximum size of characters entitled.

Step 5: Name of the table

When closing the window for defining the fields, Access asks for the name you want to give to that table.

Step 6: Primary Key

A primary key is a table field that uniquely identifies a record. The DNI in a table of people is the most typical case that is usually mentioned to explain this concept: it indisputably identifies a single individual and cannot be repeated, so it is the primary key of a table of these characteristics. It is not mandatory to define a primary key.

Step 7: Main window

Once the table has been defined, its name appears in the application's main window, as seen in the image.

Step 8: Enter the data

By double-clicking on the table's name, in the main window, a table is displayed through which it is possible to enter records. All changes are saved immediately without the need to keep them.

Creating a query

Before studying the syntax of SQL statements, it is necessary to see how you can create a query with Access.

Step 1: Main application window

In the menu on the left, select the "Queries" button and click on the "Create a query in Design view" option.

Step 2: Selection of the tables involved

The Access application has a wizard to perform queries. Although it can be convenient, we aim to learn how to develop these queries using the SQL language.

Introduction to SQL

SQL

Structured Query Language (SQL) is a standardized database language used by the Microsoft Jet database engine. SQL is used to create QueryDef objects, as the source argument to the OpenRecordSet method, and as the RecordSource property. Of data control. It can also be used with the Execute method to create and manipulate Jet databases and pass-through SQL queries to manipulate remote client-server databases.

SQL Components

The SQL language comprises commands, clauses, operators, and aggregate functions. These elements are combined in the instructions for creating, updating, and manipulating the databases.

There are two types of SQL commands:

- DLLs allow you to create and define new databases, fields, and indexes.
- DMLs will enable you to generate queries to sort, filter, and extract data from the database.

It has become a standard database language supported by most systems, from personal computer systems to mainframe computers.

As its name indicates, SQL allows us to query the database. But the term falls short since SQL performs database definition, control, and management functions. SQL statements are classified according to their purpose, giving rise to three 'languages' or rather sublanguages:

The DDL (Data Description Language) data definition language includes orders to define, modify or delete the tables in which the data is stored and the relationships between them. (It is the one that varies the most from one system to another)

The DCL (Data Control Language), data control language, contains valuable elements for working in a multi-user environment, in which data protection, table security, and the establishment of access restrictions are essential, as well as elements to coordinate the sharing of data by concurrent users, ensuring that they do not interfere with each other.

The DML (Data Manipulation Language), data manipulation language, allows us to retrieve the data stored in the database and also includes commands to allow the user to update the database by adding new data, deleting old data, or modifying previously stored data.

Language Features

An SQL statement is like a sentence in which we say what we want and where to get it.

All sentences begin with a verb (a reserved word that indicates the action to be performed), followed by the rest of the clauses, some mandatory and others optional, that complete the sentence.

Chapter 2: Data Definition Language (DDL)

A data definition language (DDL) is a language provided by the database management system that allows users of the database to carry out the tasks of defining the structures that will store the data as well as the procedures or functions that would enable them to be consulted.

The definition of the database structure includes the initial creation of the different objects that will form the database and the maintenance of that structure. DDL statements use verbs that are repeated for other objects. For example, to create a new object, the verb will be CREATE and then the type of object to make. CREATE DATABASE is the sentence to create a database, CREATE TABLE allows us to create a new table, and CREATE INDEX creates a new index... To eliminate an object, we will use the DROP verb (DROP TABLE, DROP INDEX...) and modify something in the definition of an already created object; we use the verb ALTER (ALTER TABLE, ALTER INDEX...).

The main functionalities of SQL as a definition language (DDL) are the creation, modification, and deletion of the tables that make up the database, as well as indexes, views, synonyms, permissions, etc., that could be defined on them. This document introduces the commands for essential work with tables.

- CREATE TABLE: Create a table
- SHOW TABLES: show tables
- DROP TABLE <table name>: Drop table
- DESCRIBE <table name> Show the structure of a table

CREATE DATABASE nbDatabase

```
[ ON
    [ PRIMARY ] [ <file_esp> [ , ... n ]
    [ , <group> [ , ... n ] ]
    [ LOG ON { < file_esp > [ , ... n ] } ]
    ]
    [ COLLATE nbcollation ]
    [ WITH <external_access_option> ]
]
[;]
```

As we can see, the minimum instruction is: CREATE DATABASE nbDatabase

nbDatabase: The new database's name must be exclusive within an instance of SQL Server and follow the rules for identifiers. It can have a maximum of 128 characters, except in one case we will see later.

CREATE DATABASE creates a database with the provided name. To use it, you need permission from the database.

CREATE DATABASECREATE

DROP DATABASE

DROP {DATABASE | SCHEMA} [IF EXISTS]db_name

DROP DATABASE deletes all tables in the database and deletes the database. Be very careful with this command! To use it, you need permission from the database. DROP DATABASE DROP

If you write DROP DATABASE on a symbolically linked database, both the link and the database are deleted.

DROP DATABASE returns the number of tables that are removed. Corresponds to the number of files.

The command will withdraw from the database directory the files and directories that MySQL can create during normal operations: DROP DATABASE

- All files with these extensions:

.BAK	.DAT	.HSH
.MRG	.MYD	.ISD
.MYI	.db	.frm

- All subdirectories with names that have two hexadecimal digits 00- ff. They are subdirectories used by tables RAID.
- The file DB.opt, if it exists.

If other directories or files persist in the database directory after MySQL deletes the listed files, the database directory cannot be deleted. In this case, you must delete any remaining files manually and rerun the command.

- DROP DATABASE
- CREATE TABLE and DROP TABLE
- CREATE TABLE statement

A ubiquitous CREATE command is the CREATE TABLE. Typical usage is:

CREATE [TEMPORARY] TABLE [table name] ([column definitions]) [table parameters].

DROP statement

STATEMENT TO DELETE THE TABLE.

DROP TABLE TABLE_NAME;

CREATE TABLE creates a table with the provided name. You must have permission to CREATE to the table.

By default, the table is formed in the current database. If the table exists, an error occurs if there is no current database or if the database does not exist.

The SQL syntax to CREATE TABLE is

CREATE TABLE "table_name"

("column 1" "data_type_for_column_1",

"column 2" "data_type_for_column_2",

...);

So if we need to create a table for the customer as specified above, we would enter

CREATE TABLE Customer

```
(First_Name char(50),

Last_Name char(50),

Address char(50),

City char(50),

Country char(25),

Birth_Date datetime);
```

DROP TABLE deletes one or more tables. It would help if you had permission to DROP for each table. All data in the table definition is deleted, so be careful with this command.

Sometimes we decide that we need to drop a table in the database. It would be an issue if we couldn't do it, as this would create a maintenance nightmare for DBAs. Fortunately, SQL allows us to do this since we can use the DROP TABLE command. The syntax for DROP TABLE is

DROP TABLE "table_name";

So, if we want to delete a table named customer that we created in the CREATE TABLE section, we enter

DROP TABLE Customer;

DROP TABLE can never be used to drop a table with a FOREIGN KEY constraint. First, the FOREIGN KEY constraint must be removed from the referenced table.

When a table is dropped, its rules and default values are no longer bound, and all constraints associated with it are automatically dropped. If you recreate a table, you'll need to rebind the appropriate rules and defaults and add any necessary conditions.

The DROP TABLE statement cannot be used on system tables.

ALTER TABLE and ALTER COLUMN

ALTER TABLE

The SQL ALTER TABLE command modifies a table's definition (structure) by changing its columns' definition. The ALTER command is used to perform the following functions.

1) Adding, Dropping, and Modifying Table Columns
2) Adding and removing constraints
3) Enabling and disabling constraints

The syntax for adding a column

ALTER TABLE table_name ADD column_name datatype;

For example: To add an "experience" column to the employee table, the query will be like

ALTER TABLE employee ADD experience number(3);

The syntax for removing a column

ALTER TABLE table_name DROP column_name;

For example: To remove the "location" column from the employee table, the query will be like

ALTER TABLE employee DROP location;

Syntax to modify a column

ALTER TABLE table_name MODIFY column_name datatype;

For example: To modify the salary column in the table employee, the query should be like

ALTER TABLE employee MODIFY salary number(15,2);

ALTER COLUMN

Requires that the named column is to be changed or modified.

The modified column cannot be any of the following:

- timestamp data type.">A column with a timestamp data type.
- The ROWGUIDCOL column of the table.
- A computed column or used in a calculated column.
- varchar, nvarchar, or varbinary data type is not changed, and the new size is equal to or greater than the old size, or if the column is changed from not null to null.">Used in generated statistics by the CREATE STATISTICS statement unless the column is of data type varchar, nvarchar, or varbinary; the data type is not changed. The new size is equal to or greater than the old size, or the column is changed from NOT NULL to NULL. Remove the Statistics first with the DROP STATISTICS statement Statistics generated automatically by the query optimizer are automatically removed with ALTER COLUMN.
- A column used in a PRIMARY KEY or [FOREIGN KEY] REFERENCES constraint.
- A column used in a CHECK or UNIQUE constraint. However, changing the length of a variable-length column in a CHECK or UNIQUE condition is allowed.
- A column associated with the default definition. However, a column's length, precision, or scale can be changed if the data type is not changed.
- Text, ntext, and image columns can be changed only in the following ways: ">The data type of the text, ntext, and image columns can be changed in the following ways:
- text to varchar(max), nvarchar(max), or xml">text to varchar(max), nvarchar(max) or xml
- ntext to varchar(max), nvarchar(max), or xml">ntext to varchar(max), nvarchar(max) or xml
- image to varbinary(max)">image to varbinary(max)

Chapter 3: Data Manipulation Language (DML)

Data Manipulation Language (DML) is a language provided by database management systems that allow its users to carry out the tasks of consulting or modifying the data contained in the Databases. of the Database Management System. Today, the most popular data manipulation language is SQL, used to manipulate and retrieve data in a relational database. Other examples of DML are those used by IMS/DL1, CODASYL, or other databases.

 **Data Manipulation Language Elements**

Select, Insert, Delete and Update

DML Classification

They are classified into two large groups:

- Procedural query languages *instructions*

Procedural languages. In this language, the user instructs the system to perform a series of procedures or operations in the database to calculate a final result.

- non-procedural query languages *preferences*

In non-procedural languages, the user describes the desired information without a specific procedure to obtain that information.

The database management system provides a data manipulation language (Data Manipulation Language, or DML) that allows users to query or manipulate data organized by the suitable data model.

1- INSERT

An SQL INSERT statement inserts one or more records to one (and only one) table in a relational database.

Example 1 (I insert Pepe student values in the subject spd2 to the table studied):

INSERT INTO "crusade" ("student", "subject") VALUES ("Pepe", "spd2")

2- UPDATE

An SQL UPDATE statement is used to modify the values of a set of existing records in a table.

Example 1 (I modify the subject where the student is Pepe):

UPDATE "coursed" SET "subject"= "spd3" WHERE "student"= "Pepe"

3- DELETE

A DELETE statement of SQL deletes one or more existing records in a table.

Example 1 (I delete all the values of the student and subject columns where the subject is spd2):

DELETE FROM "taken" WHERE "subject"= "

Select

What do we use SQL commands for? The everyday use is selecting data from tables in a database. Right away, we see two keywords: we need to SELECT the data FROM a table. (Note that the table is a container in the database where the data is stored. For more information about manipulating tables, see the Table Manipulation Section .) Therefore we have the most basic SQL structure:

Store_Name	you go out	txn_date
the Angels	1500	05-Jan-1999
San Diego	250	07-Jan-1999
the Angels	300	08-Jan-1999
Boston	700	08-Jan-1999

SELECT "column_name" FROM "table_name";

To illustrate the previous example, suppose we have the following table:

Store_InformationTable _

Result:
Store_Name
the Angels
San Diego
the Angels
Boston

We can use this table as an example throughout the reference guide (this table will appear in all sections). To select all businesses in this table, we enter,

SELECT Store_Name FROM Store_Information;

Multiple column names can be selected, as well as numerous table names. The SELECT indicates that we want to visualize and obtain records and results. With the FROM, we suggest from were, basically from which table, and finally, the optional were, to indicate any particular condition.

Select = Select; FROM = from, from this place; WHERE = where, that meets, (condition)

Suppose we want to know all the banned users and see how that data is saved.

- If you open the user table, you will see that it has a column called user group id (you can select * from the user to see it)
- We know that the banned User Group is 8
- Therefore, if the primary group is 8 in the user table, it is because it is banned.

The query would be:

Code: SELECT * FROM user WHERE usergroupid=8

INSERT

InsertInto

In previous sections, we have seen how to get information from tables. But how do you get these rows of data into these tables in the first place? This is covered in this section, which explains the INSERT statement, and in the next section, which explains the UPDATE statement.

In SQL, there are fundamentally two ways to INSERT data into a table: the first is to insert one row at a time, and the other is to enter multiple rows at a time. Let's first look at how we can INSERT data through one row at a time:

The syntax for inserting data one by one row at a time in a table is as follows:

```
INSERT INTO "table_name" ("column1", "column2", ...)
VALUES ("value1", "value2", ...);
```

Assuming that we have a table with the following structure,

Store_InformationTable _

And now, we want to insert into a table an additional row representing the sales data for Los Angeles on January 10, 1999. On that day, this business had $900 in sales. Therefore, we will use the following SQL script:

Column Name	Data Type
Store_Name	char(50)
you go out	float
txn_date	DateTime

```
INSERT INTO Store_Information(Store_Name, Sales, Txn_Date)
VALUES('Los Angeles', 900, '10-Jan-1999');
```

The second type of INSERT INTO allows us to insert multiple rows into a table. Unlike the previous example, where we inserted a single row by specifying its values for all the columns, we now use the SELECT statement to identify the data we want to insert into the table. If you are wondering if this means you are using information from another table, you are correct. The syntax is as follows:

```
INSERT INTO "table1" ("column1", "column2", ...)
SELECT "column3", "column4", ...
FROM "table2";
```

Note that this is the simplest form. The entire statement can easily contain WHERE, GROUP BY, and HAVING clauses, unions, and aliases.

So, for example, if we want to have a Store_Information table, which collects the sales information for the year 1998, and you already know where the data source resides in the Sales_Information table, we will enter:

```
INSERT INTO Store_Information(Store_Name, Sales, Txn_Date)
SELECT Store_Name, Sales, Txn_Date
FROM Sales_Information
WHERE Year(Txn_Date) = 1998;
```

Here we have used the SQL Server syntax to extract the annual information utilizing a date. Other relational databases may have different syntaxes. For example, in Oracle, you would use TO_CHAR(Txn_Date, 'yyyy') = 1998.

UPDATE "table_name"
SET "column_1" = [new value]
WHERE "condition";

Once data is in the table, we might need to modify it. To do so, we use the UPDATE command. The syntax for this is,

For example, let's say we currently have the table below:

Store_InformationTable _

And we noticed that the sales for Los Angeles on 08/01/1999 are €500 instead of €300, and that particular entry needs to be updated. To do so, we use the following SQL:

UPDATE Store_Information

SET Sales = 500
WHERE Store_Name = 'Los Angeles'
AND Txn_Date = '08-Jan-1999';

The resulting table would look like

Store_InformationTable _

Store_Name	you go out	txn_date
the Angels	1500	05-Jan-1999
San Diego	250	07-Jan-1999
the Angels	300	08-Jan-1999
Boston	700	08-Jan-1999

In this case, only one row satisfies the condition in the WHERE clause. If multiple rows fulfill the requirement, all of them will be modified.

It is also possible to UPDATE multiple columns at the same time. The syntax, in this case, would look like the following:

UPDATE "table_name"
SET colon 1 = [[value1], colon 2 = [value2]
WHERE "condition";

The UPDATE statement is used to modify values in a table.

The SQL UPDATE syntax is:

UPDATE table_name SET column1 = value1,
column2 = value2 WHERE column3 = value3

The SET clause sets the new values for the indicated columns.

The WHERE clause is to select the rows that we want to modify.

Note: If we omit the WHERE clause, it will default change the values in all the table rows.

Example of using SQL UPDATE

If we want to change the surname2 'BENITO' to 'RODRIGUEZ,' we will execute the:

UPDATE people SET lastname2 = 'RODRIGUEZ' WHERE firstname = 'ANTONIO' AND lastname1 = 'GARCIA' AND lastname2 = 'BENITO'

Store_Name	you go out	txn_date
the Angels	1500	05-Jan-1999
San Diego	250	07-Jan-1999
the Angels	500	08-Jan-1999
Boston	700	08-Jan-1999

Now the 'people' table will look like this:

Yam	last name 1	Surname 2

ANTONY	PEREZ	GOMEZ
LEWIS	LOPEZ	PEREZ
ANTONY	GARCIA	RODRIGUEZ
PEDRO	RUIZ	GONZALEZ

Delete From

Sometimes we may wish to get rid of the records in a table. To do this, we use the DELETE FROM command. The syntax for this is,

DELETE FROM "table_name"

WHERE "condition";

It is easier to use an example. For example, let's say we currently have the following table:

Store_InformationTable _

Store_Name	you go out	txn_date
the Angels	1500	05-Jan-1999
San Diego	250	07-Jan-1999
the Angels	300	08-Jan-1999
Boston	700	08-Jan-1999

And we decided not to keep any information about Los Angeles in this table. To achieve this, we enter the following SQL:

DELETE FROM Store_Information

WHERE Store_Name = 'Los Angeles';

Now the content of the table would look like this,

Store_InformationTable _

Store_Name	you go out	txn_date
San Diego	250	07-Jan-1999
Boston	700	08-Jan-1999

Chapter 4: Formulation of Queries with SQL

The three clauses and the construction questions in query clauses in SQL and how they relate to the construction questions:

1- SELECT clause: Where we indicate the fields of the table that we want to obtain, separated by commas. Answer the question: What data are they asking us for?
2- FROM clause: Where we indicate in which table these fields are located. Answer the question: Where is the data?
3- WHERE clause: Where we establish the condition that the records of the table that will be selected must meet. Answer the question: What requirements must the documents meet? It is where the record filter is established, that is, which records will be considered to display their data and which will not.

How is a summary query executed internally?

- First, the data source table is formed according to the FROM clause,
- the rows are selected from the data source according to the WHERE clause,
- the groups of rows are developed according to the GROUP BY clause,
- one row is obtained for each group in the resulting table with the values that appear in the GROUP BY, HAVING, and select list clauses,
- rows are selected from the resulting table according to the HAVING clause,
- columns that do not appear in the resulting table are removed from the resulting table select list,
- the rows of the resulting table are sorted according to the ORDER BY clause

A query becomes a summary query as soon as a GROUP BY, HAVING, or column function appears.

↦ field list

In a summary query, the select list and HAVING clause can only contain the following:

- constant values
- column functions
- grouping columns (columns that appear in the GROUP BY clause)
- or any expression based on the above.

GROUP BY

The corresponding SQL syntax is,

SELECT "name1_column", SUM("name2_column")

FROM "name_table"

GROUP BY "name1-column";

Let's illustrate using the following table,

Store_InformationTable _

Store_Name	you go out	txn_date
the Angels	1500	05-Jan-1999
San Diego	250	07-Jan-1999
the Angels	300	08-Jan-1999
Boston	700	08-Jan-1999

We want to calculate the total sales for each business. To do so, we would enter,

SELECT Store_Name, SUM(Sales)

FROM Store_Information

GROUP BY Store_Name;

→ typo

Store_Name	SUM(Sales)
the Angels	1500 1800
San Diego	250
Boston	700

Result:

The GROUP BY keyword is used when selecting multiple columns from a table (or tables), and at least one arithmetic operator appears in the SELECT statement. When this happens, we need to GROUP BY all other selected columns, that is, all columns except the one(s) that are operated on by an arithmetic operator.

ORDER BY

we need to enumerate the result in a particular order. This could be in ascending order, in descending order, or could be based on numeric or text values. In such cases, we can use the ORDER BY keyword to achieve our goal.

The syntax for an ORDER BY statement is as follows:

```
SELECT "column_name"
FROM "table_name"
[WHERE "condition"]
ORDER BY "column_name" [ASC, DESC];
```

[ ] means that the WHERE statement is optional. However, if a WHERE clause exists, it comes before the ORDER BY clause. ASC means that the results will be displayed in ascending order, and DESC implies that the results will be displayed in descending order. If none is specified, the default setting is ASC.

It is possible to sort by more than one column. In this case, the ORDER BY clause above becomes

ORDER BY "column_name1" [ASC, DESC], "column_name2" [ASC, DESC]

Assuming we choose ascending order for both columns, the result will be displayed in ascending order based on column 1. If there is a relationship for the value in column 1, it will be displayed in ascending order based on column 2.

For example, we might want to list the contents of the Store_Information Table by dollar amount, in descending order:

Store_InformationTable

Store_Name	~~you go out~~ SALES	txn_date
the Angels	1500	05-Jan-1999
San Diego	250	07-Jan-1999
San Francisco	300	08-Jan-1999
Boston	700	08-Jan-1999

Result:

Store_Name	~~you go out~~ SALES	txn_date
the Angels	1500	05-Jan-1999
Boston	700	08-Jan-1999
San Francisco	300	08-Jan-1999
San Diego	250	07-Jan-1999

```
SELECT Store_Name, Sales, Txn_Date
FROM Store_Information
ORDER BY Sales DESC;
```

In addition to the column name, we could use the column position (based on the SQL query) to indicate which column we want to apply for the ORDER BY clause. The first column is 1, the second is 2, and so on. In the example above, we will achieve the same results with the following command:

```
SELECT Store_Name, Sales, Txn_Date
FROM Store_Information
ORDER BY 2 DESC;
```

HAVING

The HAVING clause allows us to select rows from the table resulting from a summary query.

For the selection condition, you can use the same comparison tests described in the WHERE clause, you can also write compound conditions (joined by the OR, AND, and NOT operators), but there is a restriction.

Only the following can appear in the selection condition:

- constant values
- column functions
- grouping columns (columns that appear in the GROUP BY clause)
- or any expression based on the above.

Example: We want to know the offices with an average sales of their employees greater than 500,000 pts.

SELECT office

FROM employees

GROUP BY office

HAVING AVG(sales) > 500000

NOTE: To obtain what is requested, you have to calculate the average sales of the employees in each office, so you have to use the employee's table. We have to group the employees by the office and calculate the average for each office; finally, all that remains is to select from the result the rows with an average of more than 500,000 pts.

The resolution of the SQL UNION commands to combine the results of two queries. In this sense, UNION is similar to Join because both are used for related information across multiple tables. One restraint of UNION is that all the same columns need to contain data with similar data types. Also, when we use UNION, only discrete values are selected (identical to SELECT DISTINCT).

The syntax is as follows:

[SQL Statement 1]

UNION

[SQL Statement 2];

txn_date
05-Jan-1999
07-Jan-1999

Suppose we have the following two tables,

Store_InformationTable _

Store_Name	you go out	txn_date
the Angels	1500	05-Jan-1999
San Diego	250	07-Jan-1999
the Angels	300	08-Jan-1999
Boston	700	08-Jan-1999

Internet_Sales table

txn_date	you go out
07-Jan-1999	250
10-Jan-1999	535
11-Jan-1999	320
12-Jan-1999	750

And we want to know all the dates for a sale operation. To do so, we use the following SQL statement:

SELECT Txn_Date FROM Store_Information

UNION

SELECT Txn_Date FROM Internet_Sales;

Result:

Please note that if we enter "SELECT DISTINCT Txn_Date" for each or both SQL statements, we will get the same result set.

BASIC STRUCTURE

The basic structure of an expression for an SQL query consists of three clauses:

08-Jan-1999	
10-Jan-1999	
11-Jan-1999	
12-Jan-1999	

- select
- DESDE
- WHERE

The SELECT clause is to list the attributes that are desired in the result of a query.

The FROM clause lists the relations to be examined in evaluating the expression.

The WHERE clause establishes involving attributes of the relations that appear in the FROM clause.

A basic SQL query has the form:

SELECT A1,A2,...,An

FROM r1,r2,...,rn

WHERE P

Where Ai = attribute (Field of the table)

RI = ratio (Table)

P = predicate (condition)

Example: Select all the names of the people who have the last name MARQUES from the person table

SELECT name

FROM person

WHERE surname = " MARQUESI"

ANSWER	NAME
1	MARTIN
2	PAUL

The result of a query is, of course, another relation. If the WHERE clause is absent, the predicate P is true. The list A1, A2,..., An can be replaced by an asterisk (*) to select all the attributes of all the relations that appear in the FROM clause, although it is not convenient to choose this last option unless it is necessary because we waste a lot of time in getting it

Alias

It is possible to rename the attributes and relations, sometimes for convenience and other times because it is necessary; for this, we use the AS clause as in the following example.

Example:

SELECT P.name AS [FIRST NAME]

FROM person P

WHERE surname = "MARQUESI"

ANSWER	FIRST NAME
1	MARTIN
2	PAUL

A couple of things are worth noting in this example. When we refer to an attribute, as in a name, we can refer to it using the relation (or the alias in this example) that the attribute belongs to, followed by a period followed the attribute. Sometimes, this notation will be necessary to remove ambiguities. The square brackets are used when we use whitespace or the character (–) in the attribute name or alias.

Using aliases on the attributes allows us to rename the attributes of the query response.

When we associate an alias with a relation, we say that we create a tuple variable. These tuple variables are defined in the FROM clause after the relation name.

A scope rule is applied to the tuple variables in queries containing subqueries. In a subquery, it is allowed to use only tuple variables defined in the same subquery or any query with the subquery.

PREDICATES AND CONNECTORS

The logical connectors in SQL are:

- AND
- OR
- NOT

The logic of these connectors is the same as in any programming language, and they are used to join predicates.

The arithmetic operations in SQL are:

- + (Add)
- − (Subtraction)
- * (Multiplication)
- / (Division)

It also includes the BETWEEN comparison operator, which is used for values between

Example: Find all the names and IDs of the people whose ID is greater than 26 million and less than 28 million

SELECT name, ID

FROM person

WHERE ID BETWEEN 26000000 and 28000000

ANSWER	YAM	ID
1	MARTIN	26125988
2	STEFANIA	27128064
3	BALM	27456224
4	BETHANY	27128765

Analogously we can use the NOT BETWEEN comparison operator.

SQL also includes a selection operator for string comparisons. Models are described using the special characters:

- The character (%) is equal to any substring
- The operator (_) is equal to any character

These patterns are expressed using the LIKE comparison operator. A common mistake is using models using the equality operator (=), a syntax error.

Example: find the names that start with the letter by or the name has exactly six characters of the relationship person

SELECT name

FROM person

WHERE (name LIKE "P%") OR (name LIKE "_ _ _ _ _ _")

Analogously we can search for inequalities using the NOT LIKE comparison operator.

ANSWER	YAM
1	MARTIN
2	PAUL
3	BALM
4	SANDRA

DUPLICATE TUPLES

Formal query languages are created on the mathematical notion of relation as a set. Therefore, duplicate tuples never appear in relations. In practice, removing duplicates takes a long time. Therefore SQL allows duplicates in relations. Thus, all the tuples will be listed in the queries, including the repeated ones.

In those cases where we want to remove the duplicates forcefully, we insert the DISTINCT keyword after the SELECT clause

Example: List all non-repeating surnames of the person's relationship

SELECT DISTINCT surname

FROM person

ASKER	SURNAME
1	MARQUES
2	SANCHEZ
3	CUISINE
4	JOY
5	BRITTE
6	ARDUL
7	MICHELLI
8	musachegui
9	SERRAT

If we look at the original table of the person relation, we will see that the last name marques appeared twice, but due to the use of DISTINCT in the query, the response relation only lists a single marque.

Set operations.

SQL includes the set operations UNION, INTERSECT, and MINUS, which operate on relations and correspond to the algebra operations union, intersection, and subtraction of sets, respectively. To carry out this operation, we must be careful that the relations have the same structures.

Now let's add a new relationship, called players, which represents the people who play soccer; its attributes will be DNI, position, and number_shirt. Suppose that this new table is formed as follows:

PLAYERS	ID	MARKET STALL	NRO_SHIRT
1	26125988	FORWARD	9
two	25485699	MEDIUM	5
3	28978845	GOALKEEPER	1
4	29789854	ADVOCATE	3

Example: Obtain all the names of the related person whose surnames are Marquesi or Serrat

SELECT name
FROM PERSON
WHERE surname = "MARQUESI"
UNION
SELECT name
FROM PERSON
WHERE surname = "SERRAT"

ANSWER	FIRST NAME
1	MARTIN
2	PAUL
3	JOHN

Example: Obtain all the DNI of those who play soccer and, in addition, are on the list of the personal relationship

SELECT ID

FROM person

INTERSECT

SELECT ID

FROM players

ANSWER	ID
1	26125988
2	25485699
3	28978845

By default, the union operation removes duplicate tuples. To retain duplicates, UNION ALL must be written instead of UNION.

membership in a set

The IN connector tests whether it is a member of a set, where the set is a collection of values typically produced by a SELECT clause. Similarly, the NOT IN connector tests for not belonging to the set

Example: Finding the names of the people who play soccer and are also in the relationship person

SELECT first name, last name

FROM person

WHERE ID IN

(SELECT ID

FROM players)

ANSWER	YAM	SURNAME
1	MARTIN	MARQUES
2	PAUL	MARQUES
3	JOHN	SERRAT

It is possible to test the membership of an arbitrary relation SQL uses the element notation to represent a tuple of n elements containing the values v1,v2,…,vn.

set comparison

In sets, the phrase > is represented in SQL by (>SOME); this could also be understood as >, and its syntax is the same as that of the IN connector. SQL also allows the comparisons (>SOME),(=SOME) (>=SOME), (ALL), which corresponds to the phrase >. Like the SOME operator, it can be written (>ALL),(=ALL) (>=ALL), (10000

ANSWER	CLUB	JUG_MOST_EXPENSIVE
1	LANUS	12000

Suppose a WHERE clause and a HAVING clause both appear in the same query; the WHERE clause predicate is applied first, and the tuples satisfying the WHERE predicate are positioned into groups by the GROUP BY clause. The HAVING clause is then applied to each group.

Modification of the database

elimination

A delete request is articulated in much the same way as a query. We are only able to delete whole tuples, and we cannot delete attribute values only.

DELETE FROM r

WHERE P

where P presents a predicate and R represents a relation. Tuples t in r for which P(t) is true are removed from r.

If we omit the WHERE clause, all the tuples of the relation r are eliminated (a sound system should seek approval from the user before executing such a devastating action).

Example: Remove all tuples from the relation person where the surname is equal to "BRITTE"

DELETE FROM person

WHERE Lastname = "BRITTE"

deleted	YAM	SURNAME	ID
1	SANDRA	BRITTE	25483669

insertion

To insert data into a relation, we specify a tuple to insert or write a query whose outcome is a set of tuples to insert. The insertion of tuples is done through the statements

INSERT INTO r1

VALUES (v1,v2,…,v)

inserted	YAM	SURNAME	ID

Example: Insert a tuple with the same values as the tuple removed in the previous example into the relation person.

| 1 | SANDRA | BRITTE | 25483669 |

INSERT INTO person

VALUES("SANDRA, " "BRITTE, " 25483669)

In this example, the values are specified for the corresponding attributes listed in the relation schema. To be able to enter the data in a different order, we could have written

INSERT INTO person(ID, NAME, SURNAME)

VALUES (25483669, "SANDRA, " "BRITTE")

updates

Sometimes we may want to change the values of a tuple without changing all the values in that tuple. For this purpose, we use the statement

UPDATE r1

SET A1 = V1, A2 = V2,…,An = Vn

WHERE P

Where r1 is the relation Ai the attribute to modify Vi, the value assigned to Ai, and P is the predicate.

Example: In the player's list, update the position of the players with the number 5 jersey and assign them the number 7 jersey.

UPDATE players

SET t-shirt_number = 7

WHERE t-shirt_number = 5

updated	ID	MARKET STALL	NRO_SHIRT
1	25485699	MEDIUM	5

Null values

It is possible that for inserted tuples, only some schema attributes are given values. The rest of the attributes are assigned to null values represented by NULL. For this, we place the keyword NULL as the attribute's value.

Example: Insert in the player's relation a player with ID = 26356312, position = defender, and who has not yet been assigned a jersey_number.

INSERT INTO players

VALUES(26356312,"DEFEND",NULL)

inserted	ID	MARKET STALL	NRO_SHIRT
1	26356312	ADVOCATE	

Definition of data

Creation

A relation in SQL is defined using the command

CREATE TABLE r(A1 D1, A2 D3,…,An Dn)

Where r represents the relation's name, each Ai is the attribute's name of the scheme of the relation r, and Di is the data type of Ai. A newly created relationship is empty. The INSERT command can be used to load the relation

Example: create the relationship injured with the attributes name, surname both of type char and time_disable of type integer

CREATE TABLE "injured.DB" (

CHARNAME(20),

LAST NAME CHAR(20),

DISABLE_TIME INTEGER)

injured   YAM   SURNAME   DISABLE_TIME

elimination

To eliminate a relation, we use the DROP TABLE r order; this order eliminates all the information about the relation taken from the database; this order is more substantial than DELETE FROM r since the latter eliminates all the tuples but does not destroy the relation, while the first yes.

Example: delete the relation person

DROP TABLE person

update

The ALTER TABLE command is used to insert attributes to an existing relation. All tuples in the relation are assigned NULL as the attribute value. The ALTER TABLE syntax is as follows:

ALTER TABLE r1 ADD A1 D1

Example: Add the first, and last name char attributes to the player's relation

ALTER TABLE players ADD NAME CHAR(20)

ALTER TABLE players ADD SURNAME CHAR(20)

Chapter 5: Main Functions in SQL

The SQL database language has built-in functions that allow you to perform calculations on the data.

The SQL language has built-in functions to do calculations on data. Functions can be divided into two groups (there are many more, depending on the database system used):

SQL aggregate functions are the functions that return a single value, calculated with the values of a column.

1. AVG() - The average of the values
2. COUNT() - The number of rows
3. MAX() - The most significant value
4. MIN() - The smallest value
5. SUM() - The sum of the values
6. GROUP BY - It is a sentence that is closely linked to the aggregate functions

SQL scalar functions are the functions that return a single value that is based on the input value.

1. UCASE() - Converts a field to uppercase.

2.   LCASE() - Convert a field from uppercase to lowercase.
3.   MID() - Abstracts characters from a text field.
4.   LEN() - Returns the length of a text field.
5.   NOW() - Returns the current system time and date.
6.   FORMAT() - Formats a format for display.

For the explanation of functions, one of the tables we are going to work with is Products :

Product ID	Product Name	description	prices	Stock
1	t-shirt	Plain Black One Size T-shirt	10	16
2	Pants	Long blue chino pants	twenty	24
3	Chap	Blue cap with the Yankees logo	fifteen	32
4	Sneakers	White and green running shoes	35	13

SQL aggregate functions

1.   AVG()

The AVG() returns the average of values in a numeric column.

SELECT AVG (nombreColumna) FROM nombreTabla;

The following SQL statement returns the average of the stock in the warehouse:

SELECT AVG (Stock) FROM Productos;

The following statement displays the ProductName and Price of the records that have a Price above the average:

SELECT NombreProducto, Precio FROM Productos

WHERE Precio > (SELECT AVG (Precio) FROM Productos);

2.   COUNT()

The COUNT() returns the number of rows that meet certain criteria:

Several values in a column (NULL values are not counted):

SELECT COUNT (nombreColumna) FROM nombreTabla;

Number of records in a table

SELECT COUNT(*) FROM nombreTabla;

Number of distinct values in a column

SELECT COUNT (DISTINCT nombreColumna) FROM nombreTable;

We are now going to use the Orders table:

OrderID	CustomerID	invoice
2. 3. 4	4	160
235	5	48
236	12	64
237	4	92

If we want to know the number of orders of customer number 4 :

SELECT COUNT (ClienteID) AS PedidosCliente4 FROM Pedidos

WHERE ClienteID=4;

If we want to calculate the number of total orders:

SELECT COUNT(*) AS PedidosTotales FROM Pedidos;

If we want to calculate the number of unique customers from the Orders table:

SELECT COUNT (DISTINCT ClienteID) AS NumeroClientes FROM Pedidos;

3. MAX()

The MAX() returns the most significant value of the selected column :

SELECT MAX (nombreColumna) FROM nombreTabla;

From the products table, we are going to take the most expensive product:

SELECT MAX (Precio) AS ProductoMasCaro FROM Productos;

4. MIN()

The MIN() returns the smallest value of the selected column :

SELECT MIN (nombreColumna) FROM nombreTabla;

From the products table, we will take the cheapest product:

SELECT MIN (Precio) AS ProductoMasBarato FROM Productos;

5. SUM()

The SUM() returns the sum of a numeric column :

SELECT SUM (nombreColumna) FROM nombreTabla;

From the products table, we are going to take the total number of products in stock :

SELECT SUM (Stock) AS ProductosTotales FROM Productos;

6. GROUP BY

The GROUP BY statement is combined with aggregate functions to group one or more columns in a result set.

SELECT nombreColumna, funcion_agregada(nombreColumna)

FROM nombreTable

WHERE nombreColumna operador valor

GROUP BY nombreColumna;

If we have the tables Products, Orders, and Customers:

Product:

Product ID	Product Name	description	prices	Stock
1	t-shirt	Plain Black One Size T-shirt	10	16
2	Pants	Long blue chino pants	twenty	24
3	Chap	Blue cap with the Yankees logo	fifteen	32
4	Sneakers	White and green running shoes	35	13

Orders:

OrderID	CustomerID	invoice

2. 3. 4	4	160
235	5	48
236	12	64
237	4	92

Clients:

CustomerID	Client name	Contact
1	Lorraine Higgins	456443552
2	Raúl González	445332221
3	carmen smith	488982635
4	Ferdinand Stewart	412436773

Let's get the number of orders placed by each customer:

SELECT Clientes.NombreCliente, Count(Pedidos.PedidoID) AS NumeroPedidos FROM Pedidos

LEFT JOIN Clientes

ON Pedidos.ClienteID=Clientes.ClienteID

GROUP BY NombreCliente;

We can use GROUP BY on more than one column:

SELECT Clientes.NombreCliente, Productos.NombreProducto, COUNT (Pedidos.PedidoID) AS NumeroPedidos

FROM ((Pedidos

INNER JOIN Clientes ON Pedidos.ClienteID=Clientes.ClienteID)

INNER JOIN Productos ON Pedidos.ProductoID=Productos.ProductoID)

GROUP BY NombreCliente, NombreProducto;

SQL scalar functions

7.   UCASE()

The UCASE() converts the value of a field to uppercase.

SELECT UCASE(columnName) FROM tableName;

If we want to get all customer names in uppercase :

SELECT UCASE (NombreCliente) AS Cliente FROM Clientes;

8.   LCASE()

The LCASE() converts the value of a field to lowercase :

SELECT LCASE (nombreColumna) FROM nombreTabla;

If we want to get all customer names in lowercase :

SELECT LCASE (NombreCliente) FROM Clientes;

9.   MID()

The MID() function extracts characters from a text field.

SELECT MID (nombreColumna, inicio [, longitud]) AS unAlias FROM nombreTabla;

The required fields are columnName and start (specifies the position where to start the extraction). The optional field is length, which specifies the number of characters to return. If omitted, it returns all characters up to the end of the text.

For example, let's extract the first four characters of ProductName from the products table :

SELECT MID (nombreProducto, 1, 4) AS ProductoCorto

From Productos;

    10.   LEN()

The LEN() returns the length of a text field.

SELECT LEN(columnName) FROM tableName;

If we want to get productName and the length of product descriptions from the Products table :

SELECT NombreProducto, LEN(Descripcion) as LongitudDescripcion

FROM Productos;

    11.   NOW()

The NOW() function returns the accurate time and date.

SELECT NOW() FROM nombreTabla;

If we want to return the ProductName and Today's Price from the Products table :

SELECT NombreProducto, Precio, Now() AS PrecioProductosHoy FROM Productos;

    12.   FORMAT()

The FORMAT() function formats how a field will be displayed.

SELECT FORMAT(nombreColumna, formato) FROM nombreTabla;

Let's show a date format from the previous example :

SELECT NombreProducto, Precio, FORMAT(Now(), 'YYYY-MM-DD') AS PrecioProductosHoy FROM Productos;

Chapter 6: Building SQL Database

Creating a database in SQL Server

In this chapter, we will learn the theory of the creation of a database in SQL SERVER superficially. Likewise, we will perform an essential practice on creating a database through the SQL Server Database manager with its graphic tool Management Studio and Transact -SQL.

Logically we must have the database server installed or, in other words: Microsoft SQL Server in any version. Usually, when installing SQL SERVER, the Management Studio tool is already included, allowing you to connect and control your SQL server from a graphical interface rather than using the command line.

Database concept

A database is a set of data that belongs to the same framework and is systematically stored for later use; in other words, a database is a "STORE" that allows us to store large amounts of information in an organized way so that we can find it later. And use it easily.

Create a database using T-SQL – CREATE DATABASE

T-SQL is the data manipulation language in SQL Server; each DBMS has its language, so if we use ORACLE, the manipulation language will be PL-SQL. However, there is a standard language called SQL, and this, although with limitations in the sense that it does not provide many functions that those of DBMS have, works in any DBMS.

T-SQL or PL-SQL is the name given to the modification of the SQL language by Microsoft and Oracle, respectively; the essence of the language is maintained, which is why there are various similarities between the two. Now we will focus on T-SQL.

We will learn how to do it through Queries:

- The first thing we do is click the New Query button (or New Query) and open a new query.
- We must create a database and then put it to use, so we write the following and execute it:

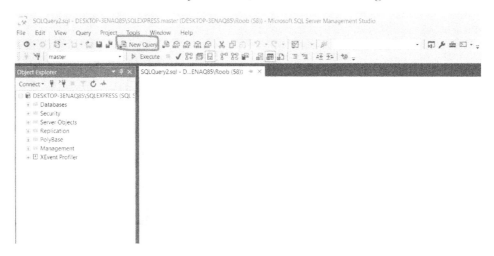

- To execute a sentence, we select it with the mouse (the whole sentence or one by one) and press the button that says " execute or run ":
- Create the database
- CREATE TOURISM DATABASE
- places the TURISMO BD in memory to be able to make modifications
- USE TOURISM

Database creation using SQL Server Management Studio

Steps to follow:

1. Connect to an instance of the SQL Server Database Engine in Object Explorer, and expand it.
2. Right-click Databases, and then click New Database.
3. 3. In New Database, specify a name for the database.
4. If you want to create a database accepting all the default values, click OK; otherwise, continue with the following optional steps.
5. Those are the steps to create a database in SQL Server graphically; finally, to reinforce what is exposed in this chapter, I share the practical video tutorial in which I carried out the database creation process using SQL Server Management Studio and Transact-SQL.
6. It is essential to mention that once we have created our empty database, we have to create the tables in which the information is stored and saved in an organized way; that will be the next topic that will be addressed on this website.

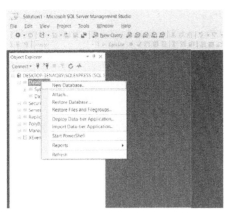

New Database

Select a page
- General
- Options
- Filegroups

Script ▾ Help

Database name: TOURISM

Owner: <default>

Use full-text indexing

Database files:

Logical Name	File Type	Filegroup	Initial Size (MB)	Autogrowth / Maxsize	Path
TOURISM	ROWS ..	PRIMARY	8	By 64 MB, Unlimited	C:\Progra
TOURISM_log	LOG	Not Applicable	8	By 64 MB, Unlimited	C:\Progra

Connection

Server:
DESKTOP-3ENAQ85\SQLEXPRES

Connection:
DESKTOP-3ENAQ85\Roob

View connection properties

Progress

Ready

Add   Remove

OK   Cancel

Book 2: Intermediate SQL

Chapter 1: How to Clone a Table in SQL Server

In some situations, we need to create an exact copy of the table with its data or structure.

When is a SQL clone required?

- When we do some testing, there is a way to change the data, so without affecting the original table, we create a copy and do all the necessary tests on this clone table.
- When we want a backup copy of the original table, we create a backing table with a clone.

In such a circumstance, we create a cloned table in SQL. This way, we save time and effort by making a new table and entering all the same information.

There are three types of clones in SQL.

1. Easy cloning

This is the easiest way to clone a table. Simple cloning requires copying data from the original table without inheriting any column attributes or indexes, creating the table, and copying the data regardless of keys and other column attributes.

Syntax:

CREATE TABLE <new_table> SELECT * FROM <original_table>;

2. Shallow cloning

Shallow cloning is generally used to duplicate the structure of a table without replicating the information. This will, so to speak, create a clone table based on the structure of the first table.

This type of cloning is done when you only need the structure and all the column attributes of the original table.

Syntax:

CREATE TABLE <new_table> LIKE <original_table>;

3. Deep cloning

Deep cloning is similar to shallow cloning, but it also copies data from the original table; that is, it inserts the data from the original table into the clone. As a result, deep cloning copies the data and the structure of the original table.

This strategy is the most widely used to create cloned tables in SQL since each property of the first table is kept the same as the records and even the auto-incrementing fields, keys, etc. We get the information replicated in the clone table from the original table.

Syntax:

CREATE TABLE <new_table> LIKE <original_table>;

INSERT INTO <new_table> SELECT * FROM <original_table>;

Summary

Cloning means copying data and structure from one table to another.

- Simple Clone - Copy the data from the original table without column attributes or indexes.

- Shallow cloning: copies only the original table structure with all column attributes and indexes. However, no table data
- Deep clone: exact as shallow clone, but also copies the source table data

Relational databases. What are it and its characteristics?

We live in an era where managing data is essential for most companies and businesses worldwide.

The world's largest technology companies, such as Netflix, Amazon, Google, and Facebook, use this information to give users what they want to see.

For this, they need to store millions and millions of data in an orderly manner so they can be extracted quickly and efficiently when required.

But how and where is this enormous amount of information stored?

Well, yes, you got it right. All this information is stored in a network of computers connected using what we know as databases (BBDD).

There are various databases, but the most widely used and the one that has been around for a long time is called a relational database.

In this chapter, you will learn what they consist of and how they work. In addition, we will give you some tips on how to start handling them.

What are relational databases?

A relational database is a database that uses the relational model to represent and create unions between different data so that it can be queried and updated using SQL (Structured Query Language).

The information is stored in tables where each one has several rows. Each of them has a unique label called the primary key.

At the same time, the table also contains columns called attributes. Each row or record in the table has associated values of its attributes. Let's take an easy example:

Imagine that we want to register the users of a website. Each user has a first name, the last name, an email, and an address.

These characteristics of each user define the table's different columns. Therefore, each user is a different row, a record in the table.

We have mentioned before that each of the records must have a unique and unique field. In this way, we can differentiate each user without any problem.

In this case, it would be the email since two users can have the same name, even the same last name, and live on the same street, but they can never have the same email.

Therefore, the user's email would be the primary key, and we could quickly identify our user.

Characteristics of relational databases

This type of database has several characteristics that make it a robust data store.

One of the main characteristics is to avoid duplication. Having duplicate elements can lead to a misinterpretation of the data.

To avoid this problem, each record is uniquely identified by a primary key. In addition, the tables must also have a unique name.

Another essential point is data integrity. This model maintains great integrity thanks to the correctness and completeness of the information, preventing data from being corrupted and new invalid entries from being added to the database.

Another peculiarity is the relationships that can be established between different tables. These relationships allow you to join and extract data from different tables as if they were one of only one.

These relationships are carried out using what are known as primary keys and foreign keys. Later we will see what these types of operations consist of.

Entity relationship model

A relational database can become very complex and have many relationships between various tables. For this reason, before starting, it is crucial to design what structure and architecture it will have.

To represent the structure, we can use what is known as the entity-relationship model. This type of representation has some elements that allow us to define all the elements of our relational database precisely. Let's see them:

Entity

Entities are a representation of objects where each one has specific characteristics. The identities are the tables that we generate in the database. To give an example, imagine an institute where we have many students.

An entity would be "students," which stores the information of each one of them. Another entity could be "exams," where the information on the exams taken during the school year is stored.

Another identity could be homework containing information on the different jobs that students have had to do at home.

These identities are represented as rectangles in the scheme or diagram we generate to determine the structure of the database.

Attributes

The attributes (columns) are the characteristics that define each element of the identity. For example, student attributes could be: age, height, grade, number of exams passed, or number of exams failed.

Each attribute gives us information about each student that contains the identity.

Relations

Relationships represent the dependencies that exist between different tables or identities. For example, each student takes different exams during the year. Therefore, each student in the "students" table or identity will be related to one or several exams in the "exams" table or identity.

Establishing this relationship, we can see a student's grades in the tests carried out during the school year.

These relationships are represented in the entity-relationship model diagram as diamonds joined to the identities by lines.

Keys

- Primary key: is a key that identifies a table entry as unique. For example, in our institute database, it would be a unique identification number for each student in the school.
- Foreign Key: This field would be, for example, the student's identifier in the exam table. In this table, the student identification will not be unique since a student takes more than one exam. Therefore, the foreign key must not be unique but related to the unique primary key of the table it is related to, in this case, the student table.

Relational Database Examples

More than examples of databases, we would have to talk about examples of relational database managers.

A database management system is a software whose function is to store, manipulate and extract all information from the database.

Some managers widely known in the technological world are the following:

1. MySQL

MySQL is the most popular open-source data management system on the planet.

Some of the advantages of MySQL are that it is free, it is a high-speed database that allows data to be consulted very quickly and accurately, it is compatible with most operating systems, and it has an encryption and security environment.

Undoubtedly, MySQL is a perfect option to implement in tools or web applications.

2. MariaDB

This manager is very similar to the previous one since it was implemented by one of the MySQL developers. These two are very similar in functionality.

However, MariaDB adds some improvements, such as the ability to perform complex queries stored in the computer's cache to improve speed when the following query is performed.

MariaDB allows the use of more complex structures, such as graph hierarchies. However, in most situations, both handlers are valid.

3. PostgreSQL

PostgreSQL, commonly called Postgres, is an open-source object-oriented data manager that works with the relational model. Its SQL language is a bit different from previous managers.

It complies with the ACID model, providing the stored data with Atomicity, Consistency, Integrity, and Durability. This prevents the stored information from being corrupted.

Advantages and disadvantages

Like most systems, the relational database has advantages and disadvantages to consider when implementing it, but, as we will see, in this case, the advantages are significant enough to make it one of the databases. Most used data, even with some deficiencies.

Advantage

Perhaps the main advantage of the relational database lies in the simplicity of the relational model, which allows for handling large amounts of data with points of relationship to each other, managing them safely, and following standards and a uniform way.

Relational databases make it possible to maintain the uniformity of the data in all the applications and copies of the database itself, called instances (for example, when we make a bank transfer and this is reflected in the bank application on our mobile in a way immediate). Relational databases ensure that all copies of the database have the same data.

In addition, relational databases guarantee, as we have already mentioned, that duplication of records does not occur. And it favors standardization by being more understandable and applicable.

Likewise, they can block such access to avoid conflicts when several users or applications try to access the same data simultaneously. In contrast, the data is being updated (such as when we are reserving numbered movie tickets).

For its part, concurrency manages calls to queries from multiple users or applications simultaneously in the same database. Through it, corrective access is provided to users or applications according to the rules or policies defined for data control.

Disadvantages

As we said, relational databases also have some disadvantages. They are mainly deficient when handling graphic data, multimedia, CAD, and geographic information systems requiring more dynamic support.

Nor do they allow you to develop hierarchically organized tables; you cannot create a sub-row because all the rows are at the same hierarchical level, and therefore you cannot use subordinate entities.

Since relational databases end up being segmented into separate tables, this causes negative performance in querying and getting the desired information.

Structure

The database is categorized into two sections: the schema and the data. The scheme defines the structure of the relational database, which stores the following data:

- The name of each table (or relation) is the set of tuples that share the same attributes: a set of rows and columns.
- The name of each column (attribute or field): is a tagged element of a tuple (such as an employee's social security number).
- The data type of each column.
- The table to which each column belongs.
- The row (tuple or record): is the data set that represents a simple object.

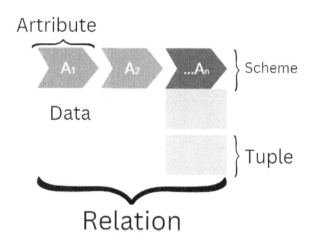

This would be the basic structure of a relational database table:

How do they work?

In relational databases, the tables are related to each other and have been previously established (that is, their structure must be previously designed). As we have already mentioned, data or records are collected in columns and rows within each table. So that the relationship between the main table and another subordinate table is established utilizing the primary or foreign keys that have been established. It is through the keys that relationships are made

For example, if the ID is ID_e and our company provides a tablet to each employee in the employee table, we will have another table that will collect the data from the tablets with an ID_t. If we include the primary key of the tablets table (ID_t) as a foreign key in the employee's table, we will relate both tables to see which tablet each employee has.

Thanks to SQL JOIN statements, it is possible to query several data tables simultaneously.

In addition, index keys allow faster access to specific data, having different combinations to consult some data or specific data.

Finally, the relationships that can be established between the different elements of two tables in a relational database can be of three types:

- One-to-one relationships when established between an entity in one table and another entity in another table.
- One-to-many relationships when established between multiple entities in one table and one entity in another table.
- Many-to-many relationships when are established between several entities of each of the tables.

Comparative relational database

Although the relational database is currently the most widely used, it does not hurt to compare it with other currently used databases. However, it will depend on the company's needs when opting for one or the other. Or the organization. Or it will even be necessary to combine different databases to obtain better results or to be able to produce more complete analyses.

vs. non-relational

A relational vs. non-relational database? When should we use one or the other type of database? Suppose we know in advance the information that we need to register. In that case, we can design the relational database structure and the tables we will need to relate them so that it is easy and fast to access the data we want to consult at any time.

A non-relational database does not have an identifier to relate one data set to another. It is usually used when the information is organized through documents or when we do not have an exact scheme of what we will store.

vs. NoSQL

What happens when I have a large volume of data to handle? Are relational databases appropriate in these cases? We face the relational database vs. NoSQL or No only SQL (not only SQL). These databases arose with the appearance of social networks and the increase in data that they entailed. In principle, they do not use the SQL language; if they do, it is only for support but not to perform the queries.

If the attributes of an element are in different columns in the relational database, in the NoSQL databases, they are grouped in the same column. To carry out the queries, they use their languages, such as JSON, CQL, or GQL. And they do not allow JOINs given the large data volume.

So if your company or business registers and stores large volumes of data, the best thing to do is opt for a NoSQL database that allows its management. In other words, relational databases fall short of big data analytics.

vs. object-oriented

The object-oriented database represents data in objects and classes; while the object can be the result of a search, the class is a collection of objects.

Thus, similar objects are grouped into a class, and each object of a particular class is called an instance. Thanks to classes, the programmer can define data not included in the program. In addition, to exchange data with each other, classes use messages called methods and have a property called inheritance, which allows a subclass to inherit properties that have been defined for a class.

This model allows you to create a superclass by combining all classes, reducing data redundancy and class reuse, and facilitating easier data maintenance. In addition, it allows you to store different types of data (audio, video, image).

Therefore, between a relational database vs. object-oriented, we must consider the needs of our company or business. Object-oriented databases seem much more helpful for fields like CAD, scientific applications, and other specific applications. However, a relational database may be sufficient for a company that only wants to have a database of its employees.

vs. transactional

Regarding the relational vs. transactional database, the truth is that the first needs the second to ensure the integrity and correctness of the data in case it is necessary to record transactions (such as online transfers from a bank or sales of an eCommerce).

Transactional databases ensure that if a system crash occurs while a transaction is in progress, the transaction will not be completed or logged, returning to the original state. Either all the steps are taken correctly, or the transaction is not completed.

Examples

Finally, we will see some relational database examples to illustrate what we have seen throughout the entry.

Suppose our company sends materials to clients first. In that case, we will have a table with the clients' information, in which each row or tuple will correspond to the data of each specific client, name, address, and billing information. The database will assign a unique key to each row, an id_c (for example),

The second table will contain information on the orders placed by customers. Each record will include the ID_c of the customer who placed the order, the product, the quantity, etc., but will not specify the name or data of the customer.

The standard data of these tables is the key, ID_c; Through this standard column, the database will establish a relationship between the two tables. Thus, each time an order is placed, the application that processes it will resort to the client's order table. The ID_c will extract the correct information about the order, the billing data, and the shipping address.

Suppose we continue with the previous example that we did with the tablets. In that case, the data in common between the table of employees and that of the tablets will be the ID_e, that is, the key that we gave to each employee so that if we want to know which tablet each employee is using, we can resort to one of the tables, that through this common data, will relate both tables. We will extract the query made as a result.

1. SQL. The query language for relational databases

Due to its efficiency, the SQL query language (Structured Query Language) has become a standard for relational databases. Despite its standardization, various extended versions have been developed commonly, such as those of Oracle or Microsoft SQL servers.

It is a declarative language in which the commands specify the result and not the way to achieve it (as occurs in procedural languages). Being declarative is systematic, simple, and has a nice learning curve. However, declarative languages lack the power of procedural ones. The great success of relational databases is partly due to the possibility of using this language. It includes various types of capabilities:

- Commands for the definition and creation of a database (CREATE TABLE).
- Commands for inserting, deleting, or modifying data (INSERT, DELETE, UPDATE).
- Commands for querying data are selected according to complex criteria involving various tables related by a common field (SELECT).
- Arithmetic capabilities: In SQL, it is possible to include arithmetic operations and comparisons, for example, $A > B + 3$.
- Mathematical functions (sqrt (x), cos (x)) or text handling.
- Assignment and print commands: It is possible to print a table built by a query or store it as a new table.
- Aggregate functions: Operations such as average (avg), standard deviation (std dev), sum (sum), maximum (max), etc., can be applied to the columns of a table to obtain a single quantity and, in turn, include it in more complex queries.

In a relational database, the query results will be individual data, tuples, or tables generated from queries in which a series of conditions based on numerical values are established. For example, a typical query on a table in a relational database using SQL could be:

```
SELECT id, name, pob1991
FROM municipalities
WHERE pop1991>20000;
```

The result will be a table in which we will have three columns (id, name, population) from the municipalities table. The rows will correspond only to those cases in which the population in 1991 (column pop1991) is more significant than 20000. In the case If only one of the municipalities met the condition, we would obtain a single row (a tuple), and if the query was:

We would obtain a single number, the population of the most populated municipality.

Designing a database in the relational model

```
SELECT pop1991
FROM municipalities
WHERE pop1991>20000;
```

A database design defines the data structure that a specific information system must have. As a general rule, phases are followed in the design process, defining the conceptual, logical, and physical model.

- In the conceptual design, a high-level description of the database structure is made, regardless of the DBMS (Database Management System) used to manipulate it. Its goal is to describe the information content of the database and not the storage structures that will be needed to handle that information.
- The logical design starts from the conceptual design and results in a description of the database structure in terms of the data structures that a DBMS can process. The logical design depends on the type of DBMS that will be used, it adapts to the technology that must be used, but it does not depend on the specific product. In the case of conventional relational databases (based on SQL to understand us), the logical design consists of defining the tables that will exist, the relationships between them, normalizing them, etc.
- The physical design starts with the logical one and results in a description of the implementation of a secondary memory database: the storage structures and the methods used to access the data efficiently. Here the objective is to achieve greater efficiency, and specific aspects of the DBMS on which it will be implemented are taken into account. As a rule, this is transparent to the user, although knowing how it is implemented helps optimize the system's performance and scalability.

The relational model

The relational model's two layers of conceptual and logical design are very similar. They are generally implemented through Entity/Relationship diagrams (conceptual model) and tables and relationships between them (logical model). This is the most common data management system model (SQL Server, Oracle, MySQL).

Note: Although many people do not know it, relational databases are called this way because they store data in the form of "Relations" or lists of data, that is, in what we usually call "Tables." Many people think that the name comes from the fact that the tables are related using foreign keys. It is not like that; it is a concept we must be clear about. (Table = Relationship) .

A few simple rules govern the relational database model:

- All the data is represented in tables (also called "relations," see previous note). Even the results of querying other tables. The table is also the central storage unit.
- The tables are made up of rows (or records) and columns (or fields) that store each of the records (information about a specific entity, considered a unit).
- The rows and columns, in principle, lack order when stored. Although in implementing each DBMS's physical design, this is not usually the case. For example, in SQL Server, if we add a key of type "Clustered" to a table, we will cause the data to be physically ordered by the corresponding field.
- The order of the columns is determined by each query (performed using SQL).
- Each table must have a primary key, a unique identifier of each record made up of one or more columns.
- To establish a relationship between two tables, it is necessary to include, in the form of a column, in one of them the primary key of the other. This column is called a foreign key. Both key concepts are fundamental in database design.

Based on these principles, the different relational databases are designed, defining a conceptual and logical design, which is then implemented in the physical design using the database manager of our choice (for example, SQL Server).

For example, consider the well-known Northwind database from Microsoft.

This database represents a simple order management system for a fictitious company. Some concepts must be handled, such as suppliers, employees, customers, transport companies, geographical regions, and orders and products.

The conceptual design of the database to handle all this information can be seen in the following figure, called the Entity/Relationship diagram or simply the ER diagram :

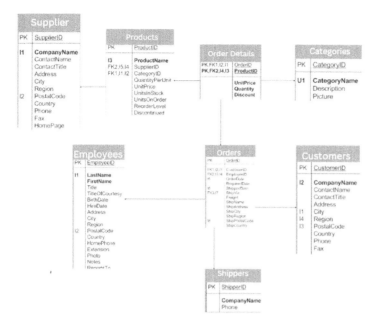

As we can see, there are tables representing each real-world entity: Suppliers, Products, Product Categories, Employees, Clients, Shippers, and Orders with their corresponding Order Details lines.

They are also related to each other so that, for example, a product belongs to a specific category (the CategoryID field relates them) and a supplier (SupplierID), the same as the other tables.

Each table has a series of fields representing values we want to store for each entity. For example, a product has the following attributes that are translated into the corresponding fields to store its information: Name (ProductName), Supplier (SupplierID, which identifies the supplier), Category to which it belongs (CategoryID), Quantity of product for each unit on sale (QuantityPerUnit), Unit price (UnitPrice), Units left in stock (UnitsInStock), Units of that product that are currently on order (UnitsOnOrder), what quantity must be for more product to be requested from the supplier (ReorderLevel) and if it is discontinued or not (Discontinued).

The fields marked with "PK" indicate those that are primary keys, that is, that uniquely identify each entity. For example, ProductID is the unique identifier of the product, which will generally be an integer that increases each time we introduce a new product (1, 2, 3, etc.).

Fields marked "FK" are foreign keys or foreign keys. They indicate fields that store the primary keys of other tables so they can be related to the current table. For example, in the products table, the CategoryID field is marked as "FK" because it will store the unique identifier of the category associated with the current product. In other words: that field will store the value of the primary key (PK) of the category table that identifies the category in which that product is.

Fields marked with indicators beginning with "I" (e.g., "I1") refer to indices. Indexes generate additional information to make finding records based on those fields easier. For example, in the employee's table (Employees), there is an "I1" index that includes the Name and Surname fields (also in bold because they will also be unique values), and that indicates that the location of customers will be facilitated utilizing These dates. It also has another "I2" index in the postal code field to quickly locate all customers in a certain area.

Fields marked with flags beginning with "U" (for example, U1) refer to fields that must be unique. For example, in the category table, the category name (CategoryName) must be unique; that is, there cannot be -logically- two categories with the same name.

As we can see, a conceptual design is nothing more than a formal and bounded representation of entities that exist in the real world and their restrictions, which are related to the domain of the problem

Logical models

Once we are clear about the ER model, we must translate it into a logical model directly in the database management system (Oracle, MySQL, SQL Server...). If we have used some professional tool to create the ER diagram, surely we can automatically generate the necessary instructions to create the database.

Most ER diagram generators (e.g., Microsoft Visio) can export the model directly to the most popular DBMS.

Then, all this conceptual model is translated into a logical one that we will transfer to the specific database we are using, which will generally be very similar. For example, this is the same model as above, already shown as tables in a SQL Server diagram:

In this case, we have created each table, one by one, following what is identified in the ER diagram and establishing indices and other elements according to the indications of each field. We have also decided the best type of data we can apply to each field (text, numbers, dates stored for each record).

Its graphical representation in the database is very similar. However, the physical model (how this is physically stored) can vary greatly from one DBMS to another, depending on the configuration we give it.

In summary

According to Thomas H. Grayson, a good database design should always have the following qualities, although some may be contradictory to each other:

- Reflect on the structure of the problem in the real world.
- Being able to represent all expected data, even over time.
- Avoid redundant information storage.
- Provide efficient access to data.
- Maintain data integrity over time.
- Be clear, coherent, and easy to understand.

As we have seen, a database design starts from a real problem we want to solve and is translated into a series of conceptual, logical, and physical models we must implement.

The first, the conceptual design, is the one that will take us the longest because we must think carefully about how we are going to represent the entities of the real world that we want to represent, what data we will store, how we will relate them to each other, etc.

The logical design is much simpler since it is nothing more than passing the previous design to a specific database. Many professional tools offer us the automatic generation of the model, so it is usually very fast.

The physical design, as a rule, falls on the database itself, based on the logical design. However, suppose we master that part well. In that case, we will carefully choose indexes, restrictions, or partitions and configurations to determine how that information will be physically stored, in what order, how it will be physically distributed in storage, etc.

SQL Insert into: To insert data

Inserting data into a table is done using the SQL INSERT INTO command. This command allows the option of including a single row in the existing database or multiple rows at once.

SQL insert command syntax

To insert data into a database, there are two main SQL insert syntaxes:

- Insert a row listing the information for each existing column (in order)
- Insert a row that specifies the columns you want to fill. It is possible to insert a row containing only part of the columns

Insert a row specifying all columns

The syntax for padding a line with this SQL insert method is as follows:

INSERT INTO table VALUES ('value 1', 'value 2', ...)

This syntax has the following advantages and disadvantages:

- Require that all data be filled in, respecting the order of the columns

- There is no column name, so typos are limited. Also, columns can be renamed without having to change the query
- The order of the columns must remain the same. Otherwise, some values risk being populated in the wrong column.

Insert a row specifying only the desired columns

This second solution is very similar, except that the name of the columns must be indicated before "VALUES." The syntax is as follows:

INSERT INTO table (colon_name_1, colon_name_2, ...

VALUES ('value 1', 'value 2', ...)

Note: It is possible not to fill in all the columns. Also, the order of the columns is not important.

Insert multiple rows at once

Multiple rows can be added to a table with a single query. To do this, the following syntax must be used:

INSERT INTO client (prenom, nom, country, age)

VALUES

('Rébeca', 'Armando', 'Mexico', 24),

('Aimée', 'Hebert', 'Mexico', 36),

('Marielle', 'Ribeiro', 'Mexico', 27),

('Hilaire', 'Savary', 'Mexico', 58);

Note: when the field to be filled is of the VARCHAR or TEXT type, it is necessary to indicate the text between single quotes. On the other hand, when the column is numeric, like INT or BIGINT, there is no need to use quotes to indicate the number.

Such an example on an empty table will create the following table:

ID	Name	Name	City	age
1	Rebeca	Arming	Mexico	24
2	Dear	Hebert	Mexico	36
3	Marielle	Ribeiro	Mexico	27
4	Hilario	savary	Mexico	58

SQL insert example

Insert into Employee

VALUES (4, 'John,' 'Fernandez,' 'Londo@hotmail.com,' 'calle5', 'Mexico,' 'Salesperson')

By checking the inserted row in the destination table, you will see that the record was inserted successfully.

Note: If your ID is inserted automatically, you do not have to specify the employee number.

To insert several records in the similar INSERT INTO statement, rather than writing multiple insert statements, we can offer the values for each row in comma-separated format, as in the T-SQL statement below that inserts three new rows into the table demo:

Insert into Employee VALUES

4	'John'	'Fernandez'	'Londo@hotmail.com'	'calle5'	'mexico'	'Salesperson'
5	'Carmen'	'Fernandez'	'Lond@ hotmail.com'	'calle1'	'mexico'	'Salesperson'
6	'Jose'	'Fernandez'	'pondo@hotmail.com'	'calle12'	'mexico'	'Seller'

| 7 | 'Mario' | 'Fernandez' | 'Lono@hotmail.com' | 'calle5' | 'mexico' | 'Seller' |

To insert values only for specific columns, we need to mention the name of these columns and offer the values for these columns in the same order as in the column list, keeping in mind that all NOT NULL columns are recorded and assigned values, as in the T-SQL statement below:

Insert into Employee VALUES

(4, 'John,' 'Fernandez,' 'Londo@hotmail.com,'' NULL,' 'Mexico,' 'Salesperson')

Note: I can add NULL as in the address field or leave it blank with the two single quotes if the table allows me to.

Conclusion

Now that you have an in-depth understanding of a relational database, you can better understand if it's the right choice for your business. As we said, the needs of the types of data you are generating and the purposes for which you want to use them will depend on it.

Relational databases can be great allies in decision-making and provide insights (valuable data) about what happens in an organization, even when it often goes unnoticed.

Chapter 2: Visualization of Data from Multiple Tables

Obtaining Data from More than One Table.

The SQL language is a very powerful and flexible tool that allows you to work with relational databases. One of the most exciting features of the SQL language is the ability to join two or more tables into one using the SELECT command and the JOIN keyword. I want to note that joining tables is a rather expensive operation, and the more rows in the table we join, the more expensive this operation is since the DBMS begins to calculate the so-called join predicate for each row. There are five types of table joins in SQL, but unfortunately, only three are implemented in SQLite.

Using UNION to join SQL queries in SQLite databases

Combining SQL SELECT queries in SQLite databases is implemented using the UNION clause, as in many other relational DBMSs. Combined SELECT queries can be considered subqueries, but that would not be entirely true. Also, don't confuse joining queries with joining tables. The JOIN keyword performs a table join operation, while a query join is performed with a UNION.

Joining SELECT queries with a UNION qualifying clause cannot be considered a SELECT subquery, if only because subqueries are normally performed on related tables, such as with a FOREIGN KEY constraint. And the union of tables by the UNION predicate is performed for tables that are unrelated in any way but with a similar structure.

TABLE A

RESULT:

Column 1	Column 2
A	A
A	B
A	C

Column 1	Column 2
B	A
A	B
B	C

TABLE B:

Column 1	Column 2
A	A
A	B
A	C
B	A
B	C

In SQLite3 databases, two options for combining queries are implemented: the first option is to use the UNION keyword, and we get non-repeating rows in the resulting table; the second option is to use the UNION ALL phrase, in which case SQLite will create the resulting table with repetitions.

The first option is somewhat slower because when executing a UNION query, SQLite compares row values. Therefore, it is important to remember that SQLite is a DBMS with dynamic data typing, in which a data class replaces the type concept. We can set the columns to an affiliated data type,

With the UNION clause, we can combine two or more queries. But it is essential to remember that for UNION to work correctly, the resulting tables of each SQL query must contain the same number of columns, with the same data type and in the same sequence. Although at the expense of data types and SQLite3 - a moot point since the data type can be converted dynamically.

Perhaps we have said everything you need to know to use the SELECT command and the UNION qualifying phrase, and now you know how query joining works in relational databases. Let's now look at examples of using SELECT and UNION.

Examples of using SELECT and UNION in SQLite3 databases. How to combine two SELECT queries

The examples of using SELECT and UNION are very simple because there is nothing complicated in joining two queries. Let's try to write a SELECT command using the UNION predicate, but first, we'll create two tables in the database using the CREATE TABLE command:

We have created two almost identical tables; the only difference is that the second has an additional age column. Both tables have column-level constraints and table-level constraints. Both tables have a PRIMARY KEY constraint, the table's index Thus, we ensured the integrity of the data in our database.

Now let's add rows to tables, for this there is an INSERT INTO command:

```
CREATE TABLE company1 (
id INTEGER PRIMARY KEY,
name TEXT NOT NULL,
pro TEXT NOT NULL,
sex TEXT NOT NULL,
sal REAL CHECK (sal > 15000));
CREATE TABLE company2 (
id INTEGER PRIMARY KEY,
name TEXT NOT NULL,
pro TEXT NOT NULL,
sex TEXT NOT NULL,
age INTEGER NOT NULL,
sal REAL CHECK (sal > 15000));
```

Adding data to the first table

```
INSERT INTO company1 (name, pro, sex, sal)
VALUES ('Pupkin Matvey', 'Dentist', 'm', 55000.00);
INSERT INTO company1 (name, pro, sex, sal)
VALUES ('Sumkin Denis', 'Lawyer', 'm', 35040.90);
INSERT INTO company1 (name, pro, sex, sal)
VALUES ('Ivanov Ivan', 'Junior Lawyer', 'm', 16000.00);
INSERT INTO company1 (name, pro, sex, sal)
VALUES ('Markova Irina', 'Accountant', 'f', 31200.10);
INSERT INTO company1 (name, pro, sex, sal)
VALUES ('Petrova Alina', 'Sales manager', 'f', 21200.10);
INSERT INTO company1 (name, pro, sex, sal)
VALUES ('Mikhailova Love', 'Secretary', 'g', 16200.10);
INSERT INTO company1 (name, pro, sex, sal)
VALUES ('Sidorova Inna', 'Head of the Service Department', 'f', 66200.10);
INSERT INTO company1 (name, pro, sex, sal)
VALUES ('Mikhailova Lyubov', 'Document Manager', 'g', 21200.10);
```

Add rows to the second table

-- note: the same lawyer works in two companies

```
INSERT INTO company2 (name, pro, sex, age, sal)
VALUES ('Petrova Valentina', 'Dentist', 'f', 41, 48000.00);
INSERT INTO company2 (name, pro, sex, age, sal)
VALUES ('Sumkin Denis', 'Lawyer', 'm', 29, 41040.90);
INSERT INTO company2 (name, pro, sex, age, sal)
VALUES ('Oleg Zamyatin', 'Junior Lawyer', 'm', 21, 19000.00);
INSERT INTO company2 (name, pro, sex, age, sal)
VALUES ('Meldonieva Veronika', 'Therapist', 'f', 33, 39200.10);
[php]
```

And now, let's combine queries using the SELECT and UNION commands:

```
SELECT * FROM company1
UNION
SELECT * FROM company2;
[/php]
```

We won't be able to join these two queries with UNION because the resulting tables have a different number of columns; let's fix that:

```
SELECT name, pro FROM company1
UNION
SELECT name, pro FROM company2;
```

Name pro
Sumkin Denis Lawyer
Markova Irina Accountant
Mikhailova Lyubov Secretary
Mikhailova Lyubov
Meldonieva Veronika Therapist
Pupkin Matvey Dentist
Petrova Alina Sales manager
Petrova Valentina Dentist
Sidorova Inna, Head of the Service Department
Zamyatin Oleg Junior lawyer
Ivanov Ivan Junior lawyer

Combining queries with row repetition: UNION ALL and SELECT in SQLite3

Pay attention to the result by combining queries; we see that lawyer Sumkin is mentioned only once; since information about him is in both the first and second tables, let's fix this by combining UNION ALL and SELECT:

```
SELECT name, pro FROM company1
UNION ALL
SELECT name, pro FROM company2;
```

name pro
Pupkin Matvey Dentist
Sumkin Denis Lawyer
Ivanov Ivan Junior lawyer
Markova Irina Accountant
Petrova Alina Sales manager

Mikhailova Lyubov Secretary
Sidorova Inna, Head of the Service Department
Mikhailova Lyubov
Petrova Valentina Dentist
Sumkin Denis Lawyer
Zamyatin Oleg Junior lawyer
Meldonieva Veronika Therapist

We have now combined the queries, and the result is a table with duplicate rows because we have combined the queries with the UNION ALL clause. There is nothing complicated about joining SQL queries in SQlite3 databases, and you need to follow the UNION rules and keep track of the data type of the columns.

JOIN and SELECT
TABLE A
TABLE B

A_id	name
1	Apple
2	Kiwi
3	Potato
4	Avocado

B_id	name
A	Apple
B	Banana
C	Avocado
D	Dill

In this chapter, we will look at the general principles of joining tables in SQL and deal with implementing the JOIN keyword using the example of databases running SQLite3. And then, we will look at each of the tables implemented in SQLite separately to understand the differences and features of internal and external joins of tables. In the course of the explanation, you will, as always, see examples demonstrating the workings of a SELECT query using JOIN.

Joining tables in SQL SELECT queries: LEFT JOIN, LEFT OUTER JOIN, INNER JOIN, CROSS JOIN.

Difference between JOIN queries.

In our opinion, JOIN queries are the most interesting thing the SELECT command can do. We have looked at joining queries in databases that are implemented using UNION. Then we will compare the selected results, but all this is not as interesting as joining tables in SQLite databases. Joining tables is done using the JOIN keyword.

The SQL standard divides table joins into three types: inner table join (INNER JOIN), outer table join (LEFT OUTER JOIN, RIGHT JOIN, FULL JOIN), and cross-table joins (CROSS JOIN). The principle of operation of any union is similar, but the results will always or almost always be different.

The principle of operation of queries to join tables in SQL and relational databases is that two or more subqueries are executed inside one SQL SELECT query (depending on how many tables we want to join), and the JOIN keyword separates the subqueries. This JOIN has an ON constraint (at least the official SQLite documentation calls it an ON constraint) called the join predicate. A join predicate is always some condition by which the RDBMS determines which rows from two tables it needs to join. But with how to combine rows, SQLite understands special modifiers: INNER, LEFT OUTER, or just LEFT and CROSS.

This explanation uses the term subquery, which is not entirely appropriate in this case; this is done intentionally to explain how JOIN works to a reader who is not yet familiar with SQL. The term subquery is not entirely appropriate since a SELECT subquery always returns some result table. When we join tables using JOIN, we often access the physical tables of the database (although no one forbids you to join an existing table with a table that will return a SELECT subquery).

In general, the SQL standard emphasizes many more JOIN modifiers:

1.   INNER JOIN - internal join of tables.
2.   LEFT JOIN or LEFT OUTER JOIN is a left outer join of tables.

3. RIGHT JOIN, or RIGHT OUTER JOIN, is a right outer join of tables.
4. FULL JOIN - the full union of tables.
5. CROSS JOIN - cross join of tables.

But in SQLite databases, there are only three types of table joins we discussed earlier; they are quite enough for any purpose. Remember when we looked at relationships between tables and tried to normalize relationships? When our database is in its first normal form, we don't even think about how to join tables in a SELECT query. Still, when a relationship is in second normal form or third normal form, we may have a question: how to get in one query data from two or three tables?

And this question is good because it is caused by laziness that saves us from stupid and unnecessary work, which forces us to improve and improve something. As you may have guessed, SELECT, combined with JOIN, saves us from the abovementioned problem.

Examples of how SELECT queries with JOIN work and diagrams showing how different ways of joining tables work

Those who have figured out how JOIN works in SQL and SQLite databases by looking at the image above - honor and praise you; it's great. Still, for those who have not figured it out, we suggest you continue reading and figuring it out, joining tables, and using JOIN in SQLite.

Preparing tables for implementing SQL JOIN query examples in an SQLite database

Let's prepare the tables to implement further examples of joining a table in a database using SQL JOIN queries. And understand the difference between LEFT JOIN, LEFT OUTER JOIN, INNER JOIN, and CROSS JOIN. Recall that in SQLite, there is no way to join tables using: RIGHT JOIN and FULL JOIN. So, let's create tables in the database using the CREATE command:

```
PRAGMA foreign_keys=on;
CREATE TABLE tracks (
id INTEGER PRIMARY KEY,
title TEXT NOT NULL,.
second INTEGER NOT NULL,
price REAL NOT NULL,
album_id INTEGER,
FOREIGN KEY (album_id) REFERENCES albums(id) ON DELETE CASCADE ON UPDATE CASCADE);
CREATE TABLE albums(
id INTEGER PRIMARY KEY,
title TEXT NOT NULL,

artist_id INTEGER,
FOREIGN KEY (artist_id) REFERENCES artist(id) ON DELETE CASCADE ON UPDATE CASCADE);
CREATE TABLE artist (id INTEGER PRIMARY KEY, name TEXT NOT NULL);
```

Three tables are linked one-to-many using a FOREIGN KEY constraint. We also ensured the integrity of the data in the database using all sorts of table- and column-level restrictions. Each table has an internal index (the ROWID column that SQLite creates automatically) and the regular one we created with the PRIMARY KEY constraint.

```
INSERT INTO artist (name)
VALUES ('Vyacheslav Butusov');
INSERT INTO artist (name)
VALUES('Spleen');
INSERT INTO artist (name)
VALUES('B-2');
```

It is worth noting that we have set the rules for cascading data update and cascading data deletion so as not to violate foreign key rules when executing data manipulation commands. Now let's add rows to the tables using the INSERT INTO command:

-- Add data to table albums

```
INSERT INTO albums (title, artist_id)
VALUES('25th frame', 2);
INSERT INTO albums (title, artist_id)
VALUES('Biography', 1);
INSERT INTO albums (title, artist_id)
VALUES('B-2', 3);
```

-- Add some albums,

-- who have neither artists nor tracks

```
INSERT INTO albums (title)
VALUES ('Fourth album');
INSERT INTO albums (title)
VALUES ('The Fifth Album');
```

-- add data to track table

```
INSERT INTO tracks (title, second, price, album_id)
VALUES ('Song of the Homecoming One', 170, 22.10, 2);
INSERT INTO tracks (title, second, price, album_id)
VALUES ('No one writes to the Colonel', 292, 32.15, 3);
INSERT INTO tracks (title, second, price, album_id)
VALUES('My friend', 291, 27.15, 3);
INSERT INTO tracks (title, second, price, album_id)
VALUES ('My heart', 249, 21.12, 1);
INSERT INTO tracks (title, second, price, album_id)
VALUES('Lifeline', 180, 41.12, 1);
INSERT INTO tracks (title, second, price, album_id)
VALUES ('We stay for the winter', 218, 17.62, 1);
```

-- Add a couple of tracks without artists

```
INSERT INTO tracks (title, second, price)
VALUES ('Dead city', 180, 41.12);
INSERT INTO tracks (title, second, price)
VALUES ('A star called the Sun', 218, 17.62);
```

We have created and filled the tables, and now we can join them using SELECT queries with the JOIN keywords in all their manifestations available in SQLite3 SQL syntax.

Internal table join in SQLite databases: INNER JOIN in SQL

Let's start with the most straightforward table join in SQL and SQLite3 databases: the inner table join. Internal table joins are implemented in SQL using the INNER JOIN keyword. An important feature of the internal join of tables in SQL SELECT queries is that the INNER JOIN qualifying phrase works symmetrically, which means that it does not matter which table will be used to the left of the INNER JOIN and which to the right.

When you want to do an internal table join in SQLite databases, you can omit the INNER keyword, as the INNER JOIN construct is the default table join in SQLite3. INNER JOIN in SQLite works quite simply: SQL SELECT query compares the rows from the left table with the rows of the right table; after comparing, SQLite3 performs a join condition check or, as they say, the join predicate is evaluated. If this calculation evaluates to TRUE, a new row will be added to the resulting table; if the result is FALSE, no row will be added to the combined table.

You can use the USING keyword in SQLite, as in many other RDBMS. The USING keyword in JOIN queries is used to enumerate a list of columns that must exist in both tables, the general syntax of USING in JOIN can be represented as:

SELECT ... FROM table1 JOIN table2 USING (column1 ,...) ...\

Joining tables INNER JOIN is the most common way to join. Let's implement a SELECT command that will use the INNER JOIN construct to join database tables:

Albums ON tracks.album_id = albums.id;

So we did an internal table join using the INNER JOIN keyword and joined the track table and the album table. In the resulting table, there are no tracks with no artists and no albums that do not have tracks, and this is very important and worth paying attention to. But note that this is not very convenient - to display all the columns of the joined tables in the result table, let's fix this:

SELECT tracks. Title, second, price, albums.title

title	second price	title
Girl in the city	193	26.2 Biography
Song of the One Who Goes Home	170	22.1 Biography
No one writes to the colonel	292	32.15 Bi-2
My friend	291	27.15 Bi-2 3
My heart	249	21.12 25th frame
Lifeline	180	41.12 25th frame
We remain in winter	218	17.62 25th frame

FROM tracks INNER JOIN

Albums ON tracks.album_id = albums.id;

id	title	second price	album_id	id	title	Artist_id
1	Girl in the city	193	26.2	2	2	Biography
2	Song of the One Who Goes Home	170	22.1	2	2	Biography
3	No one writes to the colonel	292	32.15	3	3	Bi-2
4	My friend	291	27.15	3	3	Bi-2 3
5	My heart	249	21.12	1	1	25th frame 2
6	Lifeline	180	41.12	1	1	25th frame 2
7	We remain in winter	218	17.62	1	1	25th frame

This inner table join looks more interesting, and there are no surrogate id columns. In general, if you join tables with the JOIN construct, you need to list the column names from both tables that will be displayed in the resulting table after the SELECT. Please note: if the column names are the same when joining tables, then the qualifier should be used: table_name.col_name.

We can set different data selection conditions with the WHERE clause in the case when we join tables with the JOIN predicate:

SELECT tracks.title, second, price, albums.title FROM tracks INNER JOIN

Albums ON tracks.album_id = albums.id

WHERE artist_id = 2;

In this case, we got the joined tables using INNER JOIN, selected only those columns that we wanted to see, plus filtered the data, leaving only the songs of the Spleen group. This is how the INNER JOIN construct works in SQL and SQLite3 databases.

title	second price	title

To summarize, an INNER JOIN results in a table consisting of the rows of the joined tables for which the result of the ON join predicate is TRUE. In other words: in the resulting table, there will be only those rows from the left table for which there are related rows from the right. The operation of INNER JOIN can be shown as a diagram.

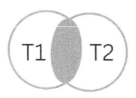

Circle T1 is the table to the left of the INNER JOIN, circle T2 is the table to the right of the INNER JOIN, and the filled area is the result table returned by the SELECT command that performs an inner table join operation.

Left join of tables in SQLite3 databases: LEFT JOIN and LEFT OUTER JOIN in SQL.

We've looked at inner table joins in SQLite databases; now, let's look at outer joins and see the difference between inner and outer joins. There is only one kind of outer join in SQLite: LEFT JOIN or LEFT OUTER JOIN.

The SQL standard defines three outer join types: LEFT JOIN, RIGHT JOIN, and FULL JOIN, but SQLite3 only has LEFT OUTER JOIN. Let's talk about the left join of tables, although it sounds more complete like this: a left outer join of tables. An outer join of tables works the same as an inner join of tables, but there is a difference in the rows output after the join predicate has been checked.

Title	second price	title
My heart	249	21.12 25th frame
Lifeline	180	41.12 25th frame
We remain in winter	218	17.62 25th frame

Let's look at an example of LEFT OUTER JOIN and, at the same time, understand the difference from INNER JOIN, as well as the peculiarity of the outer join of tables:

SELECT tracks. title, second, price, albums. title FROM tracks LEFT OUTER JOIN

Albums ON tracks.album_id = albums.id;

title second price title

title	second price	title
Girl in the city	193	26.2 Biography
Song of the One Who Goes Home	170	22.1 Biography
No one writes to the colonel	292	32.15 Bi-2
My friend	291	27.15 Bi-2 3
My heart	249	21.12 25th frame
Lifeline	180	41.12 25th frame
We remain in winter	218	17.62 25th frame
Dead City	180	41.12
A star named Sun	218	17.62

Pay attention to the results of the LEFT OUTER JOIN operation: the resulting table contains all the rows from the tracks table. Let's modify the SELECT query so that the albums table is on the left:

SELECT tracks.title, second, price, albums.title FROM albums LEFT OUTER JOIN

tracks ON albums. id = tracks.album_id;

My heart	249	21.12 25th frame
We remain in winter	218	17.62 25th frame
Lifeline	180	41.12 25th frame
Song of the One Who Goes Home	170	22.1 Biography
Girl in the city	193	26.2 Biography
My friend	291	27.15 Bi-2 3
No one writes to the colonel	292	32.15 Bi-2
Fifth album		
Fourth album		

With these two examples, we have demonstrated the difference between an inner join of a table and an outer join: between an INNER JOIN and a LEFT JOIN. SQLite evaluates the join predicate specified after the ON keyword in both cases. Still, the difference is that with a LEFT OUTER JOIN, all the left table rows will be in the resulting table, and rows of the right table will be added to them, if any. The explanation is long but clear and written in simple terms.

It can be said in another way: as a result of the LEFT OUTER JOIN operation, the table returned by SELECT will have all the rows from the left table to which the corresponding values from the right table will be added, even if these values are NULL. If it's not clear anyway, then let's present the work of LEFT OUTER JOIN in the form of a diagram:

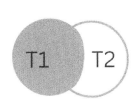

Circle T1 is the table to the left of the LEFT OUTER JOIN, and circle T2 is the table to the right of the LEFT OUTER JOIN. The resulting table in the figure is shaded. The figure shows that the resulting table will contain all the rows of the left table, and the values from the right table, if any, will be added to them.

It is worth noting that LEFT JOIN works asymmetrically, and it matters which tables will be listed first since the resulting table will contain all the rows from the first table. This is another difference between LEFT JOIN and INNER JOIN. For INNER JOIN, the order of the tables in the SQL query does not matter.

So, we have figured out the outer join of tables in SQL and have examined in detail how LEFT OUTER JOIN works in SQLite3 databases; we have also found the difference between INNER JOIN and LEFT JOIN.

Cross-join tables in SQL: CROSS JOIN in SQLite databases

We've looked at inner table joins done with INNER JOIN, and outer table joins done in SQLite databases with LEFT JOIN; now, let's move on to cross table joins done with the CROSS JOIN keyword.

A cross join of tables or CROSS JOIN is a symmetric operation, and just like INNER JOIN, the order in which the tables are written in the query does not matter; the resulting table will be the same. Cross-joining tables in mathematics is a Cartesian product, which means that as a result of the CROSS JOIN operation, SQLite will join every row of the first table with every row of the second table. As a result, we will get a table in which all combinations of possible rows are possible.

Unfortunately, it is physically impossible to demonstrate the work of CROSS JOIN on a diagram. Therefore, using an example, we will understand how the cross-join of tables works in general and SQLite databases. Let's try to write a SELECT clause using the CROSS JOIN keyword to join tables :

SELECT * FROM tracks

CROSS JOIN albums;

Here we will not present the results of the CROSS JOIN operation since we consider it not the best idea to force you to look at 45 rows of the resulting table. But we don't have to look at the values of all columns of the resulting table. We can limit them (in fact, we can limit the number of rows in the selection using LIMIT, group the selection using GROUP BY, and order the selection using ORDER BY, all this is implemented in the same way as in simple data fetch queries) and specify only the required columns, let's do this CROSS JOIN:

SELECT tracks.title, albums.title FROM tracks

CROSS JOIN albums;

We hope that you understand how CROSS JOIN works in SQLite databases and that you will have no difficulty writing a SQL query that does a cross-join of tables in a database.

Natural table join in SQL: NATURAL JOIN in SQLite

You can use the NATURAL keyword for all table join queries: NATURAL LEFT JOIN, NATURAL INNER JOIN, and NATURAL CROSS JOIN. The principle of NATURAL JOIN is very similar to that of the USING constraint, with the only difference that NATURAL JOIN automatically checks for equality between the values of each column that are in both tables:

SELECT ... FROM table1 NATURAL JOIN table2...

Something like this can describe the general syntax for using NATURAL JOIN in SQL and SQLite databases.

Examples of using NATURAL JOIN in SQLite databases:

SELECT tracks.title, second, price, albums.title FROM tracks NATURAL LEFT JOIN Albums;

SELECT tracks.title, second, price, albums.title FROM tracks INNER JOIN Albums;

The difference is that you should not evaluate ON and USING predicates when you use NATURAL JOIN, but if you do use NATURAL JOIN with ON or USING, you will get an error: a NATURAL join may not have an ON or USING clause.

Joining three or more tables in SQL and SQLite databases

The JOIN operation is very powerful but rather resource-intensive, without joining tables, it would not make sense for us to normalize relations to the second normal form or to the third normal form (how would we get summary data from related tables if there were no JOIN?), of course, we exaggerate a little. Still, table join operations make it very easy for us to work with databases.

We have already seen how two tables are joined using INNER JOIN, CROSS JOIN, and LEFT JOIN examples, and now let's see: how to combine three or more tables into one using JOIN. Everything is very simple, first an example of combining three SQL tables into one using INNER JOIN:

SELECT tracks.title, albums.title, artist.name FROM tracks INNER JOIN

Albums ON tracks.album_id = albums.id

INNER JOIN artist ON albums.artist_id = artist.id;

title	title	name
Girl in the city	Biography	Vyacheslav Butusov
Song of the One Who Goes Home	Biography	Vyacheslav Butusov
No one writes to the colonel	Bi-2	Bi-2
My friend	Bi-2	Bi-2
My heart	25th frame	Spleen
Lifeline	25th frame	Spleen
We remain in winter	25th frame	Spleen

And now an example of joining three or more SQL tables for a LEFT OUTER JOIN in an SQLite3 database :

SELECT tracks.title, albums.title, artist.name FROM tracks LEFT JOIN
Albums ON tracks.album_id = albums.id
LEFT JOIN artist ON albums.artist_id = artist.id;

title	title	name
Girl in the city	Biography	Vyacheslav Butusov
Song of the One Who Goes Home	Biography	Vyacheslav Butusov
No one writes to the colonel	Bi-2	Bi-2
My friend	Bi-2	Bi-2
My heart	25th frame	Spleen
Lifeline	25th frame	Spleen
We remain in winter	25th frame	Spleen
Dead City		
A star named Sun		

First, the first two tables will be merged, and the resulting one will be obtained, after which the resulting table will be merged with the third table, and so on indefinitely; the main thing is that values connect your tables.

To summarize, we figured out how to write SQL SELECT queries that allow us to join two or more tables into one. In the SQL language, this is done using the JOIN keyword, including in the SQLite DBMS. SQLite allows you to join tables in three ways: INNER JOIN - an inner join of tables; CROSS JOIN - a cross join of tables; and LEFT OUTER JOIN - an outer join of tables.

Chapter 3: How to use the SQL UNION operator to combine query results

The SQL UNION operator is designed to combine the resulting database tables obtained using the SELECT word. The condition for joining the resulting tables is the coincidence of the columns' number, order, and data type. ORDER BY should be applied to the result of a join and only placed at the end of a multipart query. The UNION operator has the following syntax:

SELECT COLUMNAMES (1..N) FROM TABLE_NAME UNION SELECT COLUMN_NAMES (1..N) FROM TABLE_NAME

In this construct, the merged queries may or may not have conditions in the WHERE clause. Using the UNION operator, you can combine queries to retrieve data from the same table and different ones.

When using the UNION operator without the word ALL, the result does not contain duplicates, but with the word ALL, it contains duplicates.

Totals and individual values in one table using the SQL UNION statement

With one query, you can display individual column values from the table, for example, the number of years worked by company employees, their wages, and others. With another query - using aggregate functions - you can get, for example, the amount of salaries received by employees of departments or occupying certain positions or the average number of years of work experience (in such queries, grouping is used using the GROUP BY operator).

But what if we need to get both a summary of all individual values and total values in one table? This is where the SQL UNION operator comes to the rescue, with the help of which two queries are combined. Ordering must be applied to the join result using the ORDER BY clause. Why this is necessary will be better understood from examples.

If you want to run database queries from this lesson on MS SQL Server, but this DBMS is not installed on your computer, then you can install it using the instructions on this link.

Example 1. A firm's database contains a Staff table containing data about the firm's employees. It has columns Salary (salary), Job (position), and Years (length of service). The first query returns the individual salaries sorted by position:

SELECT Name, Job, Salary FROM STAFF ORDER BY Job

The result of the query will be in the following table:

Name	job	Salary
Sanders	mgr	18357.5
Marenghi	mgr	17506.8
Pernal	Sales	18171.2
doctor	Sales	12322.4
factor	Sales	16228.7

The second query will return the total salary by position. We are already preparing this query for joining with the first one, so we will remember that a join condition is an equal number of columns, the coincidence of their names, order, and data types. Therefore, we also include the Name column with an arbitrary value of 'Z-TOTAL' in the table with totals:

SELECT 'Z-TOTAL' AS Name, Job, SUM (Salary) AS Salary FROM STAFF GROUP BY Job

The result of the query will be in the following table:

Name	job	Salary
Z-TOTAL	mgr	35864.3
Z-TOTAL	Sales	46722.3

Now let's combine the queries using the UNION operator and apply for the ORDER BY operator to the result of the union. You should group by two columns: job (Job) and name (Name), so that the rows with total (total) values, in which the name value is 'Z-TOTAL,' are below the rows with individual values. Combining query results will be as follows:

(SELECT Name, Job, Salary FROM STAFF) UNION (SELECT 'Z-TOTAL' AS Name, Job, SUM (Salary) AS Salary FROM STAFF GROUP BY Job) ORDER BY Job, Name

The result of executing a query with the UNION operator will be the following table, in which each first row in each position group will contain the total salary of employees working in this position:

Name	job	Salary
Marenghi	mgr	17506.8
Sanders	mgr	18357.5
Z-TOTAL	mgr	35864.3
doctor	Sales	12322.4
factor	Sales	16228.7
Pernal	Sales	18171.2
Z-TOTAL	Sales	46722.3

Write queries using UNION yourself and then see the solution

Example 2. The data is the same as in example 1, but the task is a bit more complicated. It is required to display in one table the individual wages sorted by positions and the total wages by positions and the total wages for all employees.

Solution. To combine with the results of the first two queries, we write a third query that returns the total salary for all employees, and it does not require grouping by position:

SELECT 'Z-TOTAL' AS Name, 'Z-ALL' AS Job, SUM(Salary) AS Salary FROM STAFF

Now let's combine queries using the UNION operator. The final request will be:

SELECT Name, Job, Salary FROM STAFF) UNION (SELECT 'Z-TOTAL' AS Name, Job, SUM(Salary) AS Salary FROM STAFF GROUP BY Job) UNION (SELECT 'Z-TOTAL' AS Name, 'Z-ALL' AS Job, SUM(Salary) AS Salary FROM STAFF) ORDER BY Job, Name

The result of this query will be the following table:

Name	job	Salary
Marenghi	mgr	17506.8
Sanders	mgr	18357.5
Z-TOTAL	mgr	35864.3
Doctor	Sales	12322.4
factor	Sales	16228.7
Pernal	Sales	18171.2
Z-TOTAL	Sales	46722.3
Z-TOTAL	Z-ALL	82586.6

Example 3. A firm's database contains a Staff table containing data about the firm's employees. It has columns Name (last name), Dept (department number), and Years (length of service).

Display in one table the average length of service by the department and the individual values of the duration of the length of service of employees, grouped by department numbers.

Solution:

The first query returns the individual lengths of seniority, sorted by department number:

SELECT Name, Dept, Years FROM STAFF ORDER BY Dept

The second query will return the average seniority by the department. A connection condition is an equal number of columns, the coincidence of their names, order, and data types. Therefore, we also include the Name column with an arbitrary value of 'Z-AVG' in the table with totals:

SELECT 'Z-AVG' AS Name, Dept, AVG(Years) AS Years FROM STAFF GROUP BY Dept

Now let's combine the queries using the UNION operator and apply for the ORDER BY operator to the result of the union. You should group by two columns: department number (Dept) and name (Name) so that rows with totals (averages) in which the value of name is NULL are higher than rows with individual values. Combining query results will be as follows:

(SELECT Name, Dept, Years FROM STAFF) UNION (SELECT 'Z-AVG' AS Name, Dept, AVG(Years) AS Years FROM STAFF GROUP BY Dept) ORDER BY Dept, Name

Name	Department	years
Sanders	twenty	7
Pernal	twenty	8
Marenghi	38	5
doctor	twenty	5
Dotor	38	8

ten	Sanders
thirty	Marenghi
100	Plotz
140	Fraye
160	Molinare
240	Daniels

The result of executing a query with the UNION operator will be the following table, in which each first row in each group of departments will contain the average length of service of employees working in this department:

Name	Department	years
Doctor	20	5.0000
Pernal	20	8.0000
Sanders	20	7.0000
Z-AVG	20	6.6667
factor	38	8.0000
Marenghi	38	5.0000
Z-AVG	38	6.5000

Other Cases of Joining Queries on the Same Table Using the SQL UNION Operator

Example 4. A Staff table in the firm's database contains data about the firm's employees. It has columns Salary (salary), Job (position), and Years (length of service). The first query is needed to get data about employees whose salary is more than 21000:

SELECT ID, Name FROM STAFF WHERE SALARY > 21000

The result of the query will be in the following table:

The second query returns the names of employees whose job title is "manager" and whose number of years of work experience is less than 8:

SELECT ID, Name FROM STAFF WHERE Job = 'Mgr' AND Years < 8 ORDER BY ID

The result of the query will be in the following table:

Now we need data that combines the selection criteria applied in the two queries. We combine queries using the UNION operator:

SELECT ID, Name FROM STAFF WHERE SALARY > 21000 UNION SELECT ID, Name FROM STAFF WHERE Job = 'Mgr' AND Years < 8 ORDER BY ID

The result of executing a query with the UNION operator will be the following table:

Category	part	Units	Money
Transport	motor vehicles	110	17600
Transport	Motorcycles	131	20960
electrical engineering	TVs	127	8255
electrical engineering	Refrigerators	137	8905
building materials	Regis	112	11760
Leisure	Music	117	7605

A query with the UNION operator can return more columns; it is important, we repeat, that the number of columns, their order, and data types match in the combined queries.

Category	part	Units	Money
Transport	motor vehicles	110	17600
Real estate	Apartments	89	18690
Real estate	Dachas	57	11970
Transport	Motorcycles	131	20960
building materials	Regis	112	11760

Example 5. There is an ad portal database.

Let's first get data about categories and parts of categories of ads that have more than 100 ads per week. We write the following query:

SELECT Category, Part, Units, Money FROM ADS WHERE Units > 100

The result of the query will be in the following table:

ID	Name
140	Fraye
160	Molinare
260	Jones

We now want to retrieve data for categories and ad category parts that generated more than 10,000 currency units per week. We write the following query:

SELECT Category, Part, Units, Money FROM ADS WHERE Money > 10000

The result of the query will be in the following table:

Now we want to retrieve data matching the criteria of the first and second queries. We combine queries using the UNION operator:

SELECT Category, Part, Units, Money FROM ADS WHERE Units > 100 UNION SELECT Category, Part, Units, Money FROM ADS WHERE Money > 10000

The result of the query will be in the following table:

ID	Name
ten	Sanders
thirty	Marenghi
100	Plotz
140	Fraye
160	Molinare
240	Daniels
260	Jones

Transport	motor vehicles	110	17600
Transport	Motorcycles	131	20960
Real estate	Apartments	89	18690
Real estate	Dachas	57	11970

electrical engineering	TVs	127	8255
electrical engineering	Refrigerators	137	8905
building materials	Regis	112	11760
Leisure	Music	117	7605

price
300
320
360
400
430

Combining Query Results on Two Tables Using the SQL UNION Operator

So far, we've looked at UNION queries that combine results from the same table. Now we will combine the results from two tables.

Example 6. There is a database of a building materials warehouse. It has a table containing wallpaper data. The Vinyl table contains data about vinyl wallpapers, and the Paper table - is about paper wallpapers. It is required to find the data on the prices of wallpapers from one table and the other.

To extract non-repeating vinyl wallpaper price data, we will create a query with the word DISTINCT:

SELECT DISTINCT Price FROM VINIL

The result of the query will be in the following table:

To retrieve non-repeated wallpaper price data, we would write the following query, also with the word DISTINCT:

SELECT DISTINCT Price FROM PAPER

The result of the query will be in the following table:

price
400
500
530
610
720
800
850

Now let's make a combined query with the UNION operator:

SELECT DISTINCT Price FROM VINIL UNION SELECT DISTINCT Price FROM PAPER

Since we are not using the word ALL, there will be no duplicate values for 400, 500, and 530. The result of the query will be in the following table:

price
300
320
360
400
430
500
530
610
720
800
850

Example 7. The database and tables are the same as in the previous example.

500
530

You want to get all price data, including recurring ones. The query to combine results using the UNION operator will be similar to the query in the previous example, but instead of just UNION, we write UNION ALL:

SELECT DISTINCT Price FROM VINIL UNION ALL SELECT DISTINCT Price FROM PAPER

The result of the query will be in the following table:

price
300
320
360
400
400
430
500
500
530
530
610
720
800
850

Using the SQL UNION operator, you can combine simple queries and queries containing subqueries (subqueries). Let's consider a corresponding example.

Example 8. There is a database called "Theater." Its Play table contains data on productions (titles - in the Name column), and in the Director table - data on directors (in the Fname column - the first name, in the Lname column - the last name). The primary key of the Director table is dir_id - the director's identification number. Dir_id is also a foreign key of the Play table and refers to the Director table's primary key. It is required to display performances directed by John Barton and Trevor Nunn.

Solution. Let's combine the results of two queries - one returns the performances of the director John Barton, the other - of Trevor Nunn. And each of these combined queries to the Play table is made with a subquery to the Director table, which returns dir_id by the name and surname of the director. Each outer query takes the value of the dir_id key from the subquery and returns the names of the productions (Name):

SELECT NAME FROM PLAY WHERE dir_id = (SELECT dir_id FROM DIRECTOR WHERE fname = 'John' AND lname = 'Barton') UNION SELECT NAME FROM PLAY WHERE dir_id = (SELECT dir_id FROM DIRECTOR WHERE fname = 'Trevor' AND lname = 'Nunn')

Chapter 4: Examples: Azure Synapse Analytics and System Analytics Platform (PDW)

Using a simple UNION statement

In the following example, the result set includes the contents of the columns CustomerKeyof the tables FactInternetSalesand DimCustomer. Since the ALL keyword is not used, duplicates are excluded from the results.

-- Uses AdventureWorks

```
SELECT CustomerKey

FROM FactInternetSales

UNION

SELECT CustomerKey

FROM DimCustomer

ORDER BY CustomerKey;
```

Using UNION with two SELECT and ORDER BY statements

When a SELECT statement in a UNION statement includes an ORDER BY clause, that clause must be placed after all SELECT statements. The following example shows the correct and incorrect use of UNION in two statements SELECT that sort a column with ORDER BY.

-- Uses AdventureWorks

-- INCORRECT	-- CORRECT

```
-- INCORRECT

SELECT CustomerKey
FROM FactInternetSales
ORDER BY CustomerKey
UNION
SELECT CustomerKey
FROM DimCustomer
ORDER BY CustomerKey;
```

```
-- CORRECT

USE AdventureWorksPDW2012;
SELECT CustomerKey
FROM FactInternetSales
UNION
SELECT CustomerKey
FROM DimCustomer
ORDER BY CustomerKey;
```

UNION of two SELECT statements with WHERE and ORDER BY

The following example shows the correct and incorrect use of UNION in two statements SELECT that require WHERE and ORDER BY.

-- Uses AdventureWorks

```
-- INCORRECT

SELECT CustomerKey
FROM FactInternetSales
WHERE CustomerKey >= 11000
ORDER BY CustomerKey
UNION
SELECT CustomerKey
FROM DimCustomer
ORDER BY CustomerKey;
```

```
-- CORRECT

USE AdventureWorksPDW2012;
SELECT CustomerKey
FROM FactInternetSales
WHERE CustomerKey >= 11000
UNION
SELECT CustomerKey
FROM DimCustomer
ORDER BY CustomerKey;
```

UNION of three SELECT statements

Using the UNION of three SELECT statements to show the effects of ALL and parentheses

In the following examples, it is used UNIONto combine results from the same table to show the properties of ALL and parentheses when using UNION.

In the first example, UNION displays duplicate records and returns each row from the source table three times. The second example uses UNIONsin ALL to remove duplicate rows from the combined results of all three statements SELECT and only returns the non-duplicate rows from the source table.

In the third example, it is used ALL with the first operation UNION and the parentheses to enclose the second operation UNION that does not use ALL. The second UNION is handled first because it is enclosed in parentheses. It only returns the unduplicated rows from the table because the option is not used; all duplicates are removed. These rows are joint with the results of the first statement SELECT using the keywords UNION ALL. In this example, duplicates between the two sets are not removed.

-- Uses AdventureWorks

```
SELECT CustomerKey, FirstName, LastName
FROM DimCustomer
UNION ALL
SELECT CustomerKey, FirstName, LastName
FROM DimCustomer
UNION ALL
SELECT CustomerKey, FirstName, LastName
FROM DimCustomer;
SELECT CustomerKey, FirstName, LastName
FROM DimCustomer
UNION
SELECT CustomerKey, FirstName, LastName
FROM DimCustomer
UNION
SELECT CustomerKey, FirstName, LastName
FROM DimCustomer;
SELECT CustomerKey, FirstName, LastName
FROM DimCustomer
UNION ALL
(
SELECT CustomerKey, FirstName, LastName
FROM DimCustomer
UNION
SELECT CustomerKey, FirstName, LastName
FROM DimCustomer
);
```

Chapter 5: Most Common Mistakes When Building Datasets in a Database

Database Design: Mistakes to Avoid and Best Practices

If the database design is done correctly, development, deployment, and subsequent performance in production will not cause many problems. A well-designed database works well, so it's important to avoid mistakes that can cause later problems for developers and database administrators.

Common flaws in database design

Among the mistakes that can be made in the database design are those related to not using stored procedures to access the data or to the lack of tests. Also, there are six serious mistakes to avoid. They are the following:

1. Lack of planning. Since the database is the cornerstone of almost all business projects, if you don't take the time to plan for the requirements of the plan and how the database is going to meet them, the entire project is likely to go off course. Also, if you don't take the time to start with the right database design, you'll find that any substantial changes to database structures that are needed to move forward could have a huge impact overall and lead to increased costs. And project delays.

2. Ignore the need for normalization. SQL was designed to work with normalized data structures. Normalization is necessary from database programming to application programming. It is extremely important not only to make development easier but also to improve performance. Indexes are very effective when they can work with the entire key value.

3. Poor naming standards. Although a personal choice, names are the first and most important line of documentation for any application. Therefore, it is necessary to ensure its consistency. The names chosen are not only to allow the purpose of an object to be identified but to allow all future programmers, users, etc., to quickly and easily understand how a part of the database was intended to be used and what data it stores. No future user should need to read a 500-page document produced at database design time to determine the meaning of some weird name.

4.   Lack of documentation. A well-designed data model adheres to a strong naming standard and contains definitions in its tables, columns, relationships, and default and check constraints. Hence, it's clear to everyone how they're intended to be used. The goal should be to provide enough information so that when the database design is complete and handed over to a support programmer, they can discover minor errors and fix them.

5.   A table to hold all domain values. Relational databases are built on the fundamental idea that each object represents one and only one thing. There should never be doubt about what a piece of data refers to. By tracing relationships, from column name to table name to primary key, it should be easy to look at them and know exactly what a piece of data means. It is, therefore, much better to avoid complexity and create robust, maintainable structures rather than trying to do as little work at the beginning of the database design project.

6.   Not protecting data integrity. All fundamental, non-changing business rules must be implemented using the relational engine. The basic rules for nullability, string length, foreign key mapping, etc., must be defined in the database. Note that there are many different ways to import data into SQL Server. If the basic rules are defined in the database itself, it can be guaranteed that they will never be overlooked. This way, queries can be written without worrying about whether or not the data being displayed complies with basic business rules.

Database design and its implementation are the cornerstone of any data-centric project and should be treated as such when it is being developed. Proper planning, normalization, strong naming standards, or documentation of your work are easy-to-apply best practices and should not be forgotten to achieve a good result. What starts well ends well.

Book 3: SQL For Data Analysis

Chapter 1: Data Manipulation

Examples of typical operators for manipulating hierarchically organized data are as follows:

- Find the specified database tree (for example, department 310);
- Jump from one tree to another;
- Jump from one entry to another within the tree (for example, from the department to the first employee);
- Move from one record to another in the order of traversal of the hierarchy;
- Insert a new record at the specified position;
- Delete the current entry.

Manipulation of the Database.

DDL instructions are used to create the database structure, the tables, and the mechanisms for accessing them. This definition language specifies the creation and destruction of database objects such as tables, views, and indexes, as well as other characteristics of databases, such as the definition of relationships, data types, etc. Some of these characteristics that allow defining a database with an adequate and complete structure to store the data will be examined below.

Integrity of entities

The primary key of a table must contain a unique, non-null value in each row. For example, the key for a Student table has a unique value for the student ID number, which uniquely identifies each student represented by a row or tuple. According to the standard, entity integrity constraints are presented through the PRIMARY KEY clause in the CREATE and ALTER TABLE statements.

This PRIMARY KEY clause must be specified only once per table. But it is still possible to ensure uniqueness for any table's alternate keys using the UNIQUE keyword. SQL will reject any attempt to perform an INSERT or UPDATE where an attempt is made to create a duplicate value within the braces.

Referential integrity

Referential integrity means that if a foreign key in a child table contains a value, that value must refer to an existing and validated row within the parent table. The definition of foreign keys is done through the FOREIGN KEY clause. When an attempt is made to delete or update a key value from the parent table with one or more corresponding rows in the child table, it depends on the specified referential action that SQL supports to make it happen: CASCADE, SET NULL, SET DEFAULT, DO NOT ACTION.

Security in the database

Data stored in the database must be protected against unauthorized access, malicious destruction or alteration, and the accidental introduction of inconsistencies that bypass integrity constraints.

Ways of malicious access include:

- Unauthorized reading of data (information theft)
- Unauthorized modification of data
- Unauthorized destruction of data
- Database security refers to protection against malicious access.

To protect the database, security measures must be adopted at various levels:

- Database system.
- Operating system.
- Net.
- Physical.

- Human

Users can have various types of authorization for different parts of the database. Among them are the following:

- Read authorization.
- Insert authorization
- The upgrade authorization.
- The authorization of deletion.

Grant of privileges.

A user who has been granted some form of approval may be authorized to pass that authorization on to other users. The SQL language offers quite a powerful mechanism for defining authorizations.

The SQL data definition language includes commands to grant and withdraw privileges. The grant statement is used to grant authorizations:

SYNTAX: Grant.

grant <privileges> on <table name> to <user list>

To revoke an authorization, the revoke statement is used. It takes a form almost identical to that of the grant, and the syntax would be:

SYNTAX: Revoke

revoke <privileges> on <table name> from <user list>

EXAMPLE.

The SQL standard includes the delete, insert, select, and update privileges. Here is a query as a practical example:

- o Privilege grant query.
- Grant select Alumni to the secretary
- Query to revoke privileges:
- Revoke the selection of Students from the secretary

CREATE clause.

CREATION OF DATABASES

The database creation process differs significantly from one product to another. A database is a named collection of objects related to each other in some way, such as tables, views, domains, etc. When creating a database, you can define its content and structure, storage space, access permissions, users it has, and a series of additional rules.

SYNTAX: CREATE A DATABASE.

CREATE DATABASE database-name

It must be taken into account that the name of the database must be a logical and acceptable name for the database manager.

CREATION OF TABLES

Once the database is created, and we are connected to it, the next thing is to create the tables that will store the data, for which it will be necessary to proceed to define the attributes of each of said columns or attributes. In addition, restrictions must be established simultaneously for every one of the attributes, as well as the creation of primary keys.

SYNTAX: CREATE A TABLE.

```
CREATE TABLE table-name
(
    attribute-name1 type options,
    attribute-name2 type options
);
```

The CREATE TABLE statement incorporates facilities for defining referential integrity and other constraints. There may be additional parameters, but the most important thing is the name we want to give to the table and the list with the definition of columns or attributes, each of which will have a name. This type will determine the kind of information that it can contain. And other options that are sometimes considered additional.

Some data types are often specific to databases but are also often a standard among programming and database administration languages, such as integer, char, float, and others.

After the data type of each column, and optionally, restrictions can be applied and keys defined. Some options are NOT NULL, UNIQUE, PRIMARY KEY, and FOREIGN KEY.

EXAMPLE.

In the following example, a new database called Library has been defined; using the reserved word USE, we directly specify the database that will be active and on which the other queries will be executed. Then we proceeded to execute the CREATE TABLE statement in which its corresponding attributes, types, and primary key have been defined. In addition, it has been specified that one of the attributes may not contain null values.

```
CREATE DATABASE Library;
USE Library;
CREATE TABLE Books
(
    IdBook INTEGER,
    ISBN VARCHAR(13) UNIQUE,
    Title VARCHAR(30) NOT NULL,
    Price INTEGER NOT NULL,
    NoEdition VARCHAR(10),
    DateEdition VARCHAR(10),
    Comments VARCHAR(50),
    CONSTRAINT pk_Books PRIMARY KEY ( bookID)
);
```

In addition, some foreign key restrictions can be specified through the statements:

CONSTRAINT FK_Books_Category FOREIGN KEY(category) REFERENCES Categories(category)

But remember that for this, you must already have the structures of the tables to be related. Therefore, the construction of all tables is recommended.

ALTER clause.

Modifications to a table can be of many types, from adding or removing a column or constraint to modifying the original definition of a column to change the type or assign or remove a default value for the column. In any of these cases, the ALTER TABLE statement must be used, followed by the table's name that will change. You must include the word ADD when you want to add a new element, ALTER when you want to modify it, or DROP if you want to delete it.

SYNTAX: ALTER

```
ALTER TABLE table-name [ADD column-name]
[ADD CONSTRAINT constraint-name]
[DROP COLUMN column-name [RESTRICT|CASCADE]]
[DROP CONSTRAINT constraint-name [RESTRICT|CASCADE]]
[ALTER COLUMN column-name]
```

In the previous syntax, the restrictions can be the following clauses: PRIMARY KEY, UNIQUE, FOREIGN KEY. The ADD COLUMN clause is very similar to the definition of a column in the CREATE TABLE statement. The DROP COLUMN clause specifies the column's name to be dropped from the table definition and can have optional qualifiers for

whether drop propagation should be cascaded.

EXAMPLE.

The ISBN attribute is removed from the book table in the first instruction. In the second, we create a new column called ISBN but with a definition of length and data type different from the

```
ALTER TABLE Books DROP COLUMN Title,
...
ALTER TABLE Books ADD Title VARCHAR,
...
ALTER TABLE Books ALTER COLUMN Title VARCHAR (45) NOT NULL,
...
ALTER TABLE Books ALTER COLUMN Price INT NOT NULL,
```

original. And the third shows how to change the definition of a column without having to delete it.

Note: To modify a UNIQUE constraint, you must delete the existing UNIQUE constraint from the object explorer under the keys or indices folder and recreate it with the new definition.

```
ALTER TABLE [database]. [Table] DROP CONSTRAINT [UNIQUE Key Name]
ALTER TABLE Books ADD ISBN VARCHAR (15) NOT NULL
```

DROP clause.

As the structure of databases changes, new tables may be created, and some others may no longer be useful. So we can remove a redundant table from the database using the DROP TABLE statement.

SYNTAX: DROP.

DROP TABLE Table name;

Create Indexes

An index is a structure that allows accelerating access to the rows of a table based on the values of one or more columns. The presence of an index significantly improves the speed of a query.

EXAMPLE.

The name of the table and the column determine the information from which the database manager will generate a new index, which it will call IndiceISBN.

CREATE INDEX Index ISBN ON Books(ISBN)

Example DBD_2.

STEP 1:

We create the database and enable its use.

Create a database Library;

use Library;

STEP 2:

We create the database's main tables, ensuring that these tables do not have any foreign keys.

```
Create table Publisher (
Code_Ed int not null,
Name_Ed varchar (50) not null,
Country_Ed varchar (30) not null,
Phone_Ed char (10),
constraint pk_Editorial primary key (Cod_Ed)
);
Create table Author (
Author_ID int not null,
Author_Name varchar (50) not null,
constraint pk_Author primary key (Author_ID)
);
Create a table Reader (
Num_Tarjetaint not null,
Reader_Name varchar (50) not null,
Reader_Address varchar (100),
Reader_Phone char (10),
DUI char (10) not null,
constraint pk_Reader primary key (Card_Num)
);
create index index_DUI on Reader(DUI);
```

STEP 3:

We create those tables that have a foreign relationship with the main tables.

```
create table Book(
Id_Libro int not null ,
Title varchar (50) not null ,
Cod_Ed int not null ,
ISBN char (10) not null ,
constraint pk_Libro primary key (Id_Libro),
constraint fk_Libro foreign key (Cod_Ed) references Publisher(Cod_Ed) on delete cascade on update cascade
);
create index index_ISBN on Book(ISBN);
create table Book_Authors(
Book_Idint not null ,
Id_Author int not null ,
constraint pk_AuthorsBook primary key (Id_Libro, Id_Author),
constraint fk1_AuthorsBook foreign key (Id_Libro) references Book(Id_Libro) on update cascade on delete cascade ,
constraint fk2_AuthorsBook foreign key (Id_Author) references Author(Id_Author) on update cascade on delete cascade
);
create table Loans(
Loan_Id int not null ,
Card_Numberint not null ,
Fecha_Salida datetime not null ,
constraint pk_Loans primary key (Id_Loan),
constraint fk_Loans foreign key (Num_Tarjeta) references Reader(Num_Tarjeta) on update cascade on delete cascade
);
```

STEP 5:

We create tables with keys made up of main tables or tables or tables with a foreign relationship.

```
create table Loan_Detail(
Loan_Id int not null ,
Book_Id int not null ,
Return_Date datetime not null ,
mora float default 0.0,
returned bit default 0,
constraint pk_LoanDetail primary key (Loan_Id, Book_Id),
constraint fk1_LoanDetail foreign key ( Loan_Id references ) on update cascade on delete cascade ,
constraint fk2_DetallePrestamo foreign key (Id_libro)references Book(Id_Libro) on update cascade on delete cascade
);
```

Chapter 2: Manipulating Data with SQL

A data manipulation command is an SQL command that modifies records. Such commands are written in the DML data manipulation language, a subset of the SQL language. These commands do not return records; they only change them in the database.

SQL DML commands are typically used to modify a large amount of data based on given criteria. For example, to increase the price of all products by 10%, use an update query, which will automatically make such changes for all products.

Visual Studio .NET provides a very powerful interface for executing DML commands. Indeed, the tools of the Visual Studio .NET environment can

deliver useful information (such as the correct connection string to connect to a database) or generate basic DML commands in the designer window when retrieving data from a table or changing the query type.

At a low level (i.e., not at the GUI level), SQL DML commands can be used with the following two tools:

- Microsoft SQL Server Query Analyzer (or simply Query Analyzer) is a GUI tool for creating queries and commands for SQL Server;
- osql is the query processor used in command line mode.

You can use any of these tools, but this chapter uses the Query Analyzer, which is more powerful and easier to use than the osql query processor. This chapter focuses on the commands executed, not on how to use the Query Analyzer GUI. The Query Analyzer tool is located in the Microsoft SQL Server program group.

Data manipulation languages in relational databases

The description of the relationship processing process can be done in two ways:

- procedural approach - by specifying operations on relations, the execution of which leads to the required result;
- declarative approach - a description of the properties the resulting relation must satisfy.

In this regard, to perform operations on relational data (data manipulation), E.F. Codd proposed two types of theoretical query languages, which are the mathematical basis of two groups of languages for operations on relations in a DBMS; these are relational algebra and relational calculus.

Relational algebra is based on applying set theory to operations on relations since relations are sets of tuples. At the same time, traditional set-theoretic operations are supplemented with special operations specific to databases. Relational algebra languages are procedural because they use a sequence of relational operators to get a query result. An example of a query language based on relational algebra is ISBL (Information System Base Language).

Predicate calculus languages are non-procedural (declarative); the query in them is built based on a first-order predicate (statement in the form of a function), which tuples or relationship domains must satisfy. A database query built in such a language does not indicate the sequence of operations that must be performed but only declares the rules for obtaining the desired result.

Codd proved that the mechanisms of relational algebra and relational calculus are equivalent: for any valid relational algebra expression, an equivalent relational calculus formula can be constructed, and vice versa. Any query that can be formulated using relational calculus can also be formulated using relational algebra and vice versa.

Both relational algebra and relational calculus have the important property of being closed concerning the concept of relation. This means that relational algebra expressions and calculus formulas are defined over relational database relations, and the calculation result is also a relation.

Both relational algebra and calculus, formulated by Codd, are theoretical languages.

Relational algebra is a set of high-level operations on relations.

One of the main characteristics of a relationship is the relationship schema, defined by the expression $R(\Lambda \vee \Lambda 2, \Lambda p)$, where R is the name of the relationship, $\Lambda v \Lambda 2$, and Λp are the names of the attributes.

The degree of a relationship is the number of its attributes. A relation of degree one is called unary, degree two - binary, degree three - ternary, ..., degree n - n-ary.

Relational algebra operations can be divided into basic set-theoretic and special relational ones.

The basic operations include the following:

- association of relations;
- the intersection of relationships;
- taking the difference of ratios (subtractions);
- the direct product of relations.

Special relational operations include:

- relationship constraint (sample);
- attitude projection;
- connection of relations;
- division of relations.

If different relations have the same attributes in the relation schema, then set-theoretic operations apply. If this condition is not met, then different relations such as join, composition, Cartesian product, and other relational algebra operations are applicable.

Subsequently, K. Date noted two shortcomings of the Codd relational algebra. The first is that the composition of operations is redundant - the minimum required to set a set of five operations: union, subtraction, product, projection, and the remaining three can be determined through these five operations. However, Codd included these operations based on the need for ease of use of the language by users of the relational database system, far from mathematics.

On the other hand, these eight operations are not enough to build databases on the principles of relational algebra.

For example, in the case of a direct product operation, if the operand relations have attributes of the same name with the same domains, a name conflict occurs: in the header (set of attribute names) of the resulting relation, the same names must appear, which contradicts the definition of a relation as a set from which it follows that all elements must be different. Renaming is introduced into relational algebra operations to solve this and other problems. It should be used when an attribute naming conflict exists in relations that are operands of the same relational operation. Then the renaming operation is applied to one of the operands first. In addition, the assignment operation is included in the composition of the algebra, which allows you to save the results of calculating algebraic expressions and some others in the database

Chapter 3: Tips and Tricks for Data Manipulation In The Database

Transform your data with R's dplyr package! Good data exploration includes data manipulation, cleaning, and summarization.

"Data scientists spend 50-80% of their time on the mundane task of collecting, manipulating, and preparing data before it can be explored for useful insights ." -NY Times.

And is that learning to manipulate, clean, and summarize your data will allow you to detect and correct incorrect, incomplete, imprecise, or unnecessary information. They are essential previous steps to know your data and propose models that explain their behavior.

For this reason, you must familiarize yourself with these processes and the tools that allow you to optimize the path. And just about the latter, I'm going to talk to you today.

Learn about the dplyr package, the flagship tool for data manipulation in R Software.

In this chapter, I will guide you to select, filter, organize, change (mutate), summarize and group your data sets with one of the most popular R Software packages. Save time and avoid errors with this super-tool you will use in all your data projects.

Also, have fun with an analysis example with the Star Wars data!

This chapter includes several tips for cleaning and transforming data using the dplyr package.

What is dplyr?

It uses a data manipulation grammar, which provides a steady set of verbs to help you solve the most common data manipulation challenges:

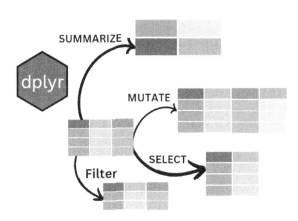

- Mutate ()   adds/changes/calculates new variables (columns).
- select()   select, chooses variables (columns) based on their names
- filter()   filters, choose observations (rows) based on their values
- summarize()   summarize, reduce multiple values to a single summary value
- arrange() sort, changes the order of the rows based on their values
- group_by() groups, performs data operations on groups defined by variables

All verbs work similarly:

1.   The first argument is a data set (data frame).
2.   Subsequent arguments describe what to do with the data frame by using variable names(without quotes).
3.   The result is a new data frame.

These properties make it easy to chain multiple simple steps together to achieve a complex result. To concatenate or join these functions, we have used the %>% pipes available through the magrittr package installed as part of dplyr. Pipes help make R expressive, like a spoken language :

"Spoken languages consist of simple words combined in sentences to create sophisticated thoughts" (Wickham & Grolemund 2014).

Read the pipes as "then" or "later." For example: "take the mtcars dataset, then group cars by transmission type, then average gas mileage."

MAKE NO CONFUSE: ggplot uses the "+" symbol instead of "%>%" to add layers to the plots.

What is special about dplyr?

1. It comprises many functions that perform joint data manipulation operations, such as applying filters, selecting specific columns, sorting data, adding or removing columns, and summarizing data.

2. It is very easy to learn and use. It is also easy to remember these functions as a filter() is used to filter rows, as its name implies.

3. The dplyr functions are processed faster than the R base functions. This is because the dplyr functions were written in a computationally efficient way. They are also more stable in syntax and better support data sets.

4. It uses the same language as other tidyverse packages, such as ggplot2, making it much easier for us.

Application of the most important functions of dplyr with data from star wars

As an example of a dplyr application, we are going to study the characters of Star Wars. The original data from SWAPI, the Star Wars API, has been revised to reflect additional research on character sex and gender determinations.

We activate the packages and observe the data

> library(dplyr)

> library(tidyr)

> data(starwars)

> starwars

The StarWars dataset is built into the dplyr package and corresponds to a dataset (a tibble) with 87 rows and 14 variables:

- name: Character name
- height: Height (cm)
- mass: Weight (kg)
- hair_color,skin_color,eye_color: Color of hair, skin, and eyes
- birth_year: Year of birth (BBY = Before the Battle of Yavin)
- sex: The biological sex of the character, that is, male, female, hermaphrodite, or neither (as in the case of droids).
- Gender: The character's gender role or gender identity is determined by their personality or how they were programmed (as in the case of droids).
- homeworld: Name of the homeworld
- species: Name of the species
- films: List of films in which the character appeared
- vehicles: List of vehicles the character has driven
- starships: List of starships the character has piloted

Filter () function: Which species are androids?

Imagine that we want to keep only the android data, we should filter the cases (rows) by the "Droid" category, and for this, we use the filter() function like this:

```
> starwars %>%
filter(species == "Droid")
>#A tibble: 6×14
> name height mass hair_color skin_color eye_color birth_year sex gender
> 1 C-3PO 167 75 gold yellow 112 none male...
> 2 R2-D2 96 32 white, blue red 33 none male...
> 3 R5-D4 97 32 white, red red NA none male...
> 4 IG-88 200 140 none metal red 15 none masculi...
> 5 R4-P17 96 NA none silver, red red, blue NA none female
> # ... with one more row, and 5 more variables: homeworld , species ,
> # films, vehicles, starships
```

Function select(): what color are the personals?

We will select those variables that indicate the character's color.

```
> starwars %>%
select(name, ends_with("color"))
> #A tibble: 87 × 4
> name hair_color skin_color eye_color
> 1 Luke Skywalker blond fair blue
> 2 C-3PO gold yellow
> 3 R2-D2 white, blue red
> 4 Darth Vader none white yellow
> 5 Leia Organa brown light brown
> # ... with 82 more rows
```

Mutate () function: Which characters are in shape?

To answer this question, we could first calculate the body mass index (BMI) with the formula BMI = mass / ((height / 100) ^ 2).

```
> starwars %>%
mutate(name, bmi = mass / ((height / 100) ^ 2)) %>%
select(name:mass, bmi)
> #A tibble: 87 × 4
> name height mass bmi
> 1 Luke Skywalker 172 77 26.0
> 2 C-3PO 167 75 26.9
> 3 R2-D2 96 32 34.7
> 4 Darth Vader 202 136 33.3
> 5 Leia Organa 150 49 21.8
> # ... with 82 more rows
```

With this information, we could only be left with cases with BMI between 18.5 and 24.9.

```
> starwars %>%
mutate(name, bmi = mass / ((height / 100) ^ 2)) %>%
select(name:mass, bmi) %>%
filter( between(bmi, 18.5, 24.9))
> A tibble: 24 × 4
> name height mass bmi
> 1 Leia Organa 150 49 21.8
> 2 Obi-Wan Kenobi 182 77 23.2
> 3 Anakin Skywalker 188 84 23.8
> 4 Chewbacca 228 112 21.5
> 5 Han Solo 180 80 24.7
> 6 Greedo 173 74 24.7
> 7 Boba Fett 183 78.2 23.4
> 8 Qui-Gon Jinn 193 89 23.9
> 9 Nute Gunray 191 90 24.7
> 10 Ben Quadinaros 163 65 24.5
> ... with 14 more rows
```

Leia and Anakin are fit!

Arrange () function: What is the smallest (least heavy) character?

```
> starwars %>%
arrange(asc(mass))
> A tibble: 87 × 14
> name height mass hair_color skin_color eye_color birth_year sex gender
> 1 Ratts T... 79 15 none grey, blue unknown NA male mascu...
> 2 Yoda 66 17 white green brown 896 male male...
> 3 Wicket ... 88 20 brown brown brown 8 male mascu...
> 4 R2-D2 96 32 NA white, bl... red 33 none mascu...
> 5 R5-D4 97 32 NA white, red red NA none male...
> 6 Sebulba 112 40 none grey, red orange NA male mascu...
> 7 Dud Bolt 94 45 none blue, gray yellow NA male mascu...
> 8 Padmé A... 165 45 brown light brown 46 fema... femin...
> 9 Wat Tam... 193 48 none green, gr... unknown NA male mascu...
> 10 Sly Moo... 178 48 none pale white NA NA NA
> ... with 77 more rows, and 5 more variables: homeworld , species ,
> films, vehicles, starships
```

Functions summarize() and group(): What is the average weight per species?

Imagine that now you want to describe the species, for example, by their average weight, and stay with those species with more than 50kg (and more than 1 case or subject).

We see, for example, that androids weigh an average of 70kg, while humans weigh 82.8.

Some final tips for data manipulation

1. Missing values. Fortunately, all aggregation functions have a na.rm argument that removes missing values before calculation.
2. Counts. Whenever you perform an aggregation, it's a good idea to include a count (n()) or a count of non-missing values (sum(!is. na(x))). That way, you can check that you're not jumping to conclusions based on very small amounts of data.
3. Ungrouping. Use ungroup if you need to remove the grouping and return to operations on ungrouped data ().

```
> starwars %>%
group_by(species) %>%
summarize(
n = n(),
mass = mean(mass, na.rm = TRUE)
) %>%
filter(
n > 1,
mass > 50
)
> #A tibble: 8 × 3
> species n mass
> 1 Droid 6 69.8
> 2 Gungan 3 74
> 3 Human 35 82.8
> 4 Kaminoan 2 88
> 5 Mirialan 2 53.1
> # ... with 3 more rows
```

Chapter 4: Database Security

Data is power for companies because they develop business opportunities, improve processes, better understand their customers and keep operating. This has made these virtual or digital pathways the object of attacks known as cybercrimes. In 2020 alone, the FBI registered 791,790 cybercrime complaints, which implies a growth of 69% compared to the previous year.

Think of it like a highway along which you transport valuable data; These are linked from one digital environment to another, and along the way, "cybernetic thieves" try to hack your information, that is, to violate the accesses to get hold of the data, which is later used for their benefit and causes substantial losses to the companies Business.

Based on data from insurers, it is estimated that the costs of cybercrime amount to USD 6 trillion annually.

Along with these hacks, various companies have specialized in developing systems and technologies for database security.

What is database security?

They are all those measures, technologies, and protocols that an organization implements to protect the data it manages and establish padlocks that prevent access to said information to unauthorized persons or entities.

The data is contained or circulating at different points, for example, on your website, in your transfers, on computers, in an email, contact records, databases, etc. The function of database security is to guarantee the privacy of these channels.

It is important to clarify that although the data moves in virtual spaces, your measures or actions can also be physical; for this reason, it is mentioned that security can come from protocols, that is, from processes that involve your collaborators and also from certain elements physical, for example, the fact that USB devices are not used in work computers.

To generate efficient database security efforts, people, protocols, and technological systems must be involved; otherwise, there will be no protection.

The importance of database security: 5 key benefits

1. Save costs – By backing up data to the cloud and distributing it across more servers on and off-premises, your organization can mitigate the risk posed by cyberattacks. Ensuring data is protected by proper security controls minimizes the chances of a cyber breach, which means cost savings. With each attack prevented, you will save an average of 682 thousand USD.
2. Builds resilient operations – Organizations with multiple servers for cloud data storage (both on and off-premise) are operationally resilient.
3. Strengthens decision-making – Better-protected data provides continuity for tracking business strategies and their day-to-day implementation.
4. Protects against ransomware attacks – Achieved by taking a proactive stance against attacks through measures such as staff training, threat hunting, and endpoint and network monitoring
5. Helps comply with data privacy laws – Complying with privacy laws and data breach policies reduces risk; At the same time, it is relevant to encourage customer trust in an environment where 38% of consumers between the ages of 16 and 25 do not trust retail companies' handling of their sensitive data.

Database security features

Information security or database protection is proactive, predictive, and reactive; that is, actions must be established to inhibit cyberattacks, as well as technologies that are continuously protecting from the source.

- It is proactive when establishing information security processes and protocols, training employees, and communicating measures.
- It is predictive because mechanisms for monitoring and analysis of possible vulnerable cases must be established. Therefore, an organization can anticipate what a hacker is looking for.
- It is reactive when the threat is imminent, and if there is a cyberattack, it reacts to avoid it, thus guaranteeing protection.

How does database protection work?

Database security will focus on critical, valuable, or sensitive information for the organization. Database security systems ensure confidentiality, integrity, availability, and authentication (a method of identifying who may have access).

Considering this, the protection of information bases works in stages that you can escalate according to your company's type of operation. That's why:

- Identify the most vulnerable data, that is, the ones that are most sensitive for the company, because this way, you will have visibility of what you want to protect.
- Analyze the routes and channels through which this data circulates since, in this way, you can locate the most critical points.
- Establish processes and protocols, so everyone handling such data knows what to do and what not to do.
- Implements access controls and authentication to the databases.
- Then you must encrypt or encrypt the information based on the information security systems or technologies you use in your company.
- Communicate, train and inform all company members about the measures continuously.
- Monitor databases, and analyze computing environments and possible vulnerabilities.
- Create an action plan in cases of threats and incidents to know how to react, stop or minimize the impacts of a cyber attack.

Now see what the most common types of database security are.

Ten types of security for databases

1. Hardware security

It has to do with all the physical devices that can contain or through which the data can transit, for example, firewalls or hardware firewalls, proxy servers, security modules for encrypted keys, and authentication systems, among others.

2. Software Security

In this case, it focuses on the virtual part, that is, on the programs, platforms, software, and applications focused on protecting information. The best-known example, in this case, is an antivirus.

3. Network security

This type of security focuses on the path through which data is transmitted, such as the cloud, to guarantee access to the data without making it vulnerable to possible theft. All kinds of defense against cyber espionage, hacking, Trojans, interception of communications, and others are concentrated here.

4. Database Backups

A specific type of security is the backup of the databases, which can be complete when all the data is copied; differentials when only data that has been modified or updated is stored; or incremental backups when added information is saved.

5. Encryption

With this, the data that, in addition to being stored, make some journey through the network is protected. If there is data theft, this type of security makes it difficult for the cybercriminal to interpret and use it.

6. Intrusion detection

This type of security is activated when the system detects someone trying to access a denied access or suspicious activity around the data. Network Intrusion Detection Systems (NIDS) continuously monitor data transit.

7. Incident management

Security information systems and event management (SIEM) visualize database security comprehensively since, through monitoring, they analyze incidents to generate reports that help manage secure information.

8. Internet protocols

Every action on the Internet poses a cyber risk because you make yourself visible, and you are in everyone's way. Therefore, this type of security seeks to protect users on the Internet through HTTPS, SSL, and TLS cybersecurity systems, which are applied so that websites are safe and users can share information or interact in these spaces.

9. Data Loss Prevention (DLP)

This type of security applies actions that guarantee that certain data is not sent from the network in such a way that it supervises and assures authorized persons that confidential data is not being copied or shared.

10. Defense in Depth

This type of security tries to cover all the routes, environments, and processes through which a company's data circulates or is stored. It will involve technologies or systems to encrypt, mask data, apply access controls, and constantly monitor and generate reports.

Eight tips for choosing the best protection for your databases

There are many types of security and protection systems for your databases and information, so you must analyze the operation of your organization to find out which are the best protection technologies. Here are some tips that can help you choose your database protection:

1. Conduct an audit

It is essential to audit the type of devices and hardware you use in your company, the software, the network, and the processes carried out in each area or work team that involves data management.

2. Create a database landscape

Based on the audit, you must create a broad overview of your databases, that is, know what they are, what type of data they contain, where they come from, and what routes they take; This way, you will be able to classify the information and identify which are the most vulnerable, critical, sensitive and confidential databases. Likewise, you will determine the routes and points you should especially reinforce.

3. Detect endpoint threats

Endpoints are those that are remotely connected to a work network. Detecting their threats helps you prevent ransomware cyberattacks as you develop positive habits in your organization and implement solutions like antivirus and data security backups.

4. Look for tools that are constantly updated

Protection programs require continuous updating because there is new information about types of viruses and attacks every day, so consider those solutions that do it constantly.

5. Seek support and advice

Along with the previous point, you need a provider that provides support and consulting, making it easier to implement solutions and their scalability. In addition, with a good consultancy, it will be easier for you to carry out the training and education of all collaborators.

6. Find masking solutions

A good practice is the anonymization or masking of the data. It implies generating a similar version based on the same structure as the original, but sensitive data is modified to protect it.

7. Avoid FTP scripts

If you use FTP scripts to communicate or exchange information, you are opening a security breach that leaves your data vulnerable since this protocol does not use encryption. Please verify that your systems have other protocols or are adequately reinforced.

8. Adapt secure internal tools

Many gaps that can alter the security of your databases come from within your organization, so it is recommended that you implement secure collaboration channels or platforms between areas, teams, and workers. Even your internal chat software is important, as are the tools you use for external clients and agents.

Five database security tools

Treat your databases as a fortress with high walls and various defenses, which you can create by implementing different tools:

- Antivirus software – All computers connected to the network should host a reliable antivirus. This software integrates different protection actions to detect malware or other malicious elements. With this, you can eliminate threats or establish a quarantine period for those devices that presented the incidents. The implemented software must have relevant updates. Antimalware and antispyware software are also implemented, whose function is to monitor and supervise traffic on the Internet.
- Network Perimeter Firewall: It is one of the most recommended cybersecurity tools, as it scans network packets and allows or blocks access based on rules defined by an administrator. Modern systems must be installed to classify the files used in various parameters.
- Proxy servers: a computer program that acts as an intermediary between the browser and internet connections by filtering all the packets between the two. This tool is classified as one of the best in computer security because it blocks websites considered dangerous or prohibited within the work environment. In addition, it establishes an authentication system, which limits access to the external network and allows having records on sites, and visits, among other data.
- Endpoint Encryption – This encrypts data so unauthorized persons cannot interpret or use it.
- Vulnerability Scanner – This software detects, analyzes, and manages vulnerable paths. It issues alerts in real-time, which helps to solve problems promptly and without compromising the continuity of operations within the organization.

Although the database protection market is constantly changing and developing in the face of new threats, the tools mentioned earlier will help you maintain the confidentiality, integrity, and availability of data during the rest and transit stages; without forgetting that with better security measures, the risk of information being stolen will be less.

Chapter 5: Combine Data Science Languages with WPS Analytics

It is often debated which data programming language a data scientist should learn. The SAS language, R, Python, SQL, Julia, and so on have their supporters and detractors. It is safe to assume that the best language is the one that helps you maximize your productivity and achieve your goals.

Organizations often have all kinds of programming language usage and experience; different areas of an organization may prefer different languages, and within an area, there may be reasons for using one language over another for different tasks.

Each language has its strengths:

- Structured Query Language (SQL)

SQL is the most popular language for interacting with databases. Simple yet powerful, it is often the starting point for people learning to analyze data. It can be a good tool for data extraction, sorting, and summarising tasks. It quickly becomes cumbersome or impractical for tasks involving heterogeneous data sources, multiple steps, or procedural programs.

- SAS Language

The SAS language facilitates simple data processing and advanced analytical tasks and allows you to process large volumes of data with a minimum of computational resources and lines of code. The SAS language provides scalable data preparation coupled with robust statistical methods. Generally, there is no restriction on how much data can fit in memory. Commercial vendors of SAS language compilers provide high levels of support for critical data and statistical library analytics environments.

- R Language

The R language has strong ad hoc visualization capabilities and allows users to perform advanced and niche statistical analysis. R has a large community of open-source contributors, which helps the range of statistical packages grow even further. However, the vast set of available libraries can be difficult to navigate. The R language generally requires data to fit in memory, which limits R's ability to handle large volumes of data. The data preparation features of the R language are not that strong.

- Python Language

Popular among students, Python is a more commonly used programming language than R or SAS. Some popular Big Data analytics libraries are written in Python, such as PySpark and its APIs for many components of the Hadoop ecosystem and Deep Learning frameworks like Theano and Tensorflow.

- Julia Language

A recent addition to the data language market, the Julia language is well-designed and can be executed efficiently.

- Other Languages

The above languages are the ones most commonly associated with data science. Data analysis is possible in various languages, including extensive libraries for numerical and statistical analysis, including Java, C, Fortran, Octave, SPSS, and many more.

Ideally, data scientists can produce programs that use the best tool for each aspect of a data science task. Imagine reading the data from your SQL database, doing a frequency analysis on a couple of lines using the frequency procedure in the SAS language, and then plotting the results with ggplot2 in R, or imagine your highly competent SAS language analysts. They can generate data preparation workflows that a new employee with optimal Python skills can use.

Switching between R and Python can sometimes be done using extensions like the rPy2 Library in Python or the rPython package in R.

In these situations, WPS is the ideal integrated data science platform that allows data scientists to use the same program to code end-to-end with SAS, R, Python, SQL, and Java within the same program. And development environment.

So, imagine we have a large dataset that contains customer data, with one of the fields being unstructured text data. Using WPS, it is possible to combine in a single script:

- SQL to interact with the database
- SAS language for data preparation and reporting
- R for text mining
- SAS language for modeling
- Python for additional modeling

The modeling example above in the SAS language predicts capital gains based on age, relationship type, years of education, and income level, creating separate models by gender.

```
Proc sort data=census;
by sex;
proc glm data=census alpha=0.5;
class relationship income;
model capital_gain=relationship age education_num income;
by sex;
run;
```

WPS Analytics Program. One program, multiple languages.

Let's assume that most customer history resides in a structured relational database. It might be ideal for reading the data directly and using the native language of the database, invoking some stored procedures that have been previously coded or pasting in a query that your DBA team has previously created. What happens if there is additional data inside a Hadoop cluster? You can connect to databases to read data with the SAS language, for example, in the SQL procedure:

```
Proc sql;
Create table customers as select*from Hadoop.customers
quit;
```

SAS language is ideal for data preparation with multiple features, including import, merge, filter, transform and reshape, missing value imputation, and validation. For example, you can modify the structure of the data set using the transpose procedure of the SAS language:

```
proc transpose data=customers;
out=custom;
var arreas1-arreas9;
by customer date;
run;
```

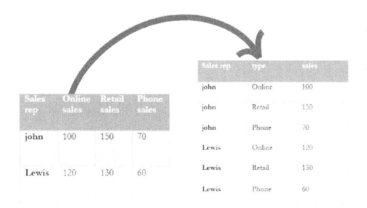

The SAS language has fewer functional features for unstructured data. The R and Python languages can take advantage of full frameworks to perform sentiment or tf-idf analysis and convert the output to a structured format for modeling. The R procedure of the SAS language makes it easy to send a data set to R, where we can derive sentiment variables:

Using a post with users and some text fields:

Username	Text
user 1	I had a horrible experience in the store; and the staff was rude, the customer service was mediocre; I will never go back
user 2	Decent service, though slow, overall good experience
user 3	I am very satisfied with your service, reliable and great value for money

This results in a sentiment score that can be used in subsequent modeling or reporting.

Username	Text	feeling
user 1	I had a horrible experience in the store; and the staff was rude, the customer service was mediocre; I will never go back	-0.963
user 2	Decent service, though slow, overall good experience	0.158
user 3	I am very satisfied with your service, reliable and great value for money	0.915

The Python language has useful modeling packages, such as Scikit-learn and Keras, a high-level API for the Tensorflow and Theano deep learning frameworks. Using the SAS language Python procedure, it is easy to take advantage of this Python functionality within the program.

```
proc python;
*Send dataset to Python;
export data=mv;
submit;
*Your python code here;
from sklearn.model selection import
train test split
from keras.layers import Dense from keras.models import Sequential
X_tr,x_ts,y_tr,y_ts =
train_test_split(mv.drop(['y'1,1),mv.y)
model = Sequential ()
model. add (Dense (100, input_shape=X_tr.shape [1]))
model.add (Dense (50, activation ='relu')) model.add (Dense (1)) model. compile (loss='mean_squared _error',
optimizer = 'adam')
model.fit(X_tr, y_tr)
scored = model.predict(X ts)
endsubmit;
*Retrieve resulting pandas dataset;
import python=scored;
run;
```

```
proc r;
*Send transpose procedure output dataset to
R; export data=custom;
submit;
*Your R code here;
library (tm)
source ("sentiment. R')
# convert to a corpus
crp < - Corpus (VectorSource (custom))
# convert to lower case, remove punctuation
crp < - tm map (crp,
content transformer (tolower))
crp < - tm map (crp, removePunctuation)
# apply sentiment function
mining_view = sentiment (crp)
endsubmit;
*Retrieve resulting R data frame;
import r=mining view;
run;
```

Using this approach with the World Programming WPS platform has some advantages:

- Analysis programs are easy to implement: a single program can be scripted or invoked via the command line.
- Easily maintainable pipelines and analytics workflows as only a single file needs to be tracked for configuration management and version control

- Different skill sets can be leveraged seamlessly using built-in libraries of best-in-class technologies. Intellectual property assets can be universally preserved and reused

It's easy to have the best of all worlds, using the most appropriate technology for each part of a single analysis process. You can balance the needs of Big Data, structured and unstructured data, data preparation, processing speed, machine learning, AI capabilities, production deployment, and financial cost without the constraints of a suite of technologies, still accessible within a Managed and consistent framework and user interface.

Chapter 6: Data Cleaning

We know that one of the biggest nightmares for your marketing and sales strategies is those terrible old email addresses, duplicate contacts, and misspelled names. This low-quality data can affect the databases within your CRM and other marketing strategies. In addition, they could derail your commercial and advertising initiatives in a more negative scenario.

Your customer data is one of your company's most important and valuable elements. Therefore, you must ensure they have the highest possible quality and present the most relevant service to your business.

You can apply a data cleansing strategy to keep everything in order in your databases. If you do not know what we mean, we will discuss its function and how to do it.

What is data cleansing or data cleansing?

As its name implies, it debugs bad data in a table or database. This action allows you to identify incorrect, incomplete, or irrelevant data for your company. After cleaning, the unusable data is replaced, modified, or completely deleted.

Data purification helps you save many hours of cleanup work. In addition, it ensures that the data you have is reliable. This assures you that any information you get from them will be much more accurate and useful for your business.

Why is data cleansing important?

Data cleansing is vital to ensure high data integrity in your business. If all the information in your organization is reliable, then you can be sure that the decisions you make based on it will be the most accurate.

The quality of data may vary depending on its quality; among the main ones are:

- Accuracy: All data within your company must be accurate. One way to check their accuracy is by comparing them with other sources. If this source does not exist or is inaccurate, then the information you have will also be inaccurate.
- Consistency: Data consistency lets you know if your contact information for a person or organization is the same across different databases, tables, or applications you use.
- Validity: all data must comply with defined rules or restrictions. In the same way, each piece of information must be able to be validated to verify if they are correct or not.
- Uniformity: All the data within your databases must have the same values or units. This is essential when doing data cleansing because the process becomes complex if you don't have everything in order.

Here are some tips for effective data cleansing to help you figure out how to have better contact data in your databases.

How to perform data cleansing

1. Say goodbye to duplicate data

Duplicate data often occurs for two reasons: first, inconsistent data entry, and second, multiple channels capturing contact information.

Some tools can help you eliminate this duplicate data. For example, Google Contacts is a free tool that merges your contacts and detects duplicates.

You may need to manually scan and edit your contacts if you've never done deduplication. Although this task may take some time, doing it right from the beginning will help ensure that new data entry meets quality requirements, and you only have to do this activity once.

- Use tools like Dedupley.
- Use email data validation tools. Experian Data Quality has programs that meet this goal. It also massively analyzes telephone numbers.
- To avoid having duplicate contacts in different apps, you can keep your main tools in sync, eliminating the need to enter the same information on different platforms or places.

2. Check the new data

Implement a comprehensive system across your business to ensure that all new and updated data is correctly entered into your central database. For example, you can verify that your team always fills out certain information fields (like name, phone number, and email) in your CRM using the same format. You can also set some requirements for a contact record to avoid missing data and everyone meeting the same information.

Another option is to synchronize contacts between your CRM and other tools. This guarantees that your management platform and other applications have the same information. In this way, you reduce the probability of errors when entering new data.

3. Keep your data up to date

Some data obtained from Data Axle indicates that around 70% of the data within a CRM becomes obsolete annually. This is due to various reasons, but the main ones are organizational changes. While for every 30 minutes, a new company is formed, and at the same time, 20 managers leave their jobs.

These internal movements entail changes in emails, telephone numbers, new positions, and others; there will be many stale contacts.

Therefore it is better to keep your data updated by implementing some tactics. One of them is to use analytics tools that scan all incoming emails and update contact information as it becomes available. If a contact changes roles or organizations, your central database can be updated instantly.

You can also remove any email addresses that have bounced or been excluded. This type of information is most likely found in your email marketing tool. This wonderful practice also supports you in staying out of spam folders.

4. Implement consistent data entry

It does not matter that you have the best data cleaning strategy if the data dump does not have good practices in your day-to-day. Make sure that all your collaborators know the data entry standards of your company. For example, ensure they know which information fields to fill out when creating a contact record, how to check for duplicate data before creating a new contact, and that they're entering data into the correct apps.

If you follow these simple tactics, you can be sure that your contact database will be impeccable. Don't forget to bi-directionally sync data between your key business applications – minimize manual data entry and ensure you're always looking for the most up-to-date and accurate contact information across all your tools.

Chapter 7: Pivot Functions

What are pivot tables?

Pivot tables allow us to classify, total, count, or give the average of a set of stored data in an automated way, which is done in the data stored in a Table (known as databases). Or a spreadsheet (in the case of Excel), among other statistical functions. The results of this stored data are exposed in a secondary information box (done within the same dynamic table) that shows all the data ordered and summarized so they can be understood.

The pivot table is a cool feature that allows you to manage data and make relationships and dependencies seem obvious. It is achieved by transforming rows into columns and arranging them the way you want.

What is a pivot or pivot table in SQL?

In SQL, a pivot or pivot table is a data set transformed from a group of rows separated by a specific set of columns. In relational databases, such as Oracle and MySQL or Microsoft SQL Server, using dynamic tables (pivot), our data can be simplified to have simple and orderly management to read and understand them. To create a pivot table, it must be taken into account that it is necessary to use an aggregate towards a data group to distribute the data in several rows of a single column; they can also be used in a single row with several columns. The implementation of these tables helps us to be able to dynamize the set of results laterally.

- Example of pivot tables in SQL

To better understand how pivot tables work, you will be shown an example containing various sales data types. You can copy the code in Microsoft SQL to test what they do.

```
Create table #PivotTestTable (CustName varchar(8), Item_Type varchar(8), Item_Amount numeric(6,2))
insert into #Pivot Test Table select 'Jason', 'Computer', 435.34 union select 'Jason', 'Software', 243.54 union select 'Jason', Monitor',
158.23 union select Alison', 'Computer', 345.89 union select Alison', 'Software 78.78 union select 'Alison', 'Monitor', 123.45
```

- Understanding non-dynamic data

When the table is of temporary type, # PivotTestTable, a query is made, and the result that it will give us will look as follows

CustName Item_Type Item_Amount

Alison Computer 345.89 Alison Monitor 123.45 Alison Software 78.78 Jason Computer 435.34 Jason Monitor 158.23 Jason Software 243.54

As you can see, we are shown the results of the two clients that have been created, Jason and Alison, and the different products they have purchased are shown. Our table will have six rows (for the products), with two columns (for our two customers). So that we can see both data in a single row for each customer, it is necessary to implement a pivot table.

- Most common errors when using pivot tables

```
SELECT p1.CustName, p1.Item_Amount as Computer, p2.Item_Amount as Monitor, p3. Item_Amount as
Software FROM #PivotTestTable p1 INNER JOIN #PivotTestTable p2 on p1.CustName = p2. CustName and
p2.Item_Type = 'Monitor' INNER JOIN #PivotTestTable p3 on p1.CustName = p3.CustName and
p3.Item_Type = 'Software' WHERE p1.Item_Type = 'Computer'
```

A recurring error when creating a pivot table is creating a new combination on the source pivot table. Performing this action could generate very unreliable or incorrect results. We will show you an example of what should not be done with a pivot table. Possibly, the result may be the same in some cases, but this example will not work in all cases.

How to master the pivot tables?

Mastering pivot tables may, at first, seem like a subject to master perfectly. However, it is necessary to have some basic principles to understand how it works. You can reach the level of experts in pivot tables quickly. Still, you must have the necessary bases and be guided by the documentation to achieve this objective.

Mastery of dynamic tables in the labor market is highly required, so mastery over them will provide a little more curricular value in labor issues.

Using the Pivot Tables

We can use a pivot table to summarize, order, group, reorganize, and count all the total or average data stored in a table. Also, it doesn't help to be able to transform columns into rows and rows into columns. We will be able to group the data by any field (column), and through operations and advanced calculations on them, we will be able to obtain specific information.

Using pivot tables to create a list of unique values is recommended. Because pivot or pivot tables help us summarize data, tables can be used to find unique values in a given column. Dynamic tables provide quick information since it allows us to recover all the values that appear in a field and detect certain typographical errors and other inconsistencies.

- We can group elements, records, and rows into categories we create.
- Count the records of a certain category in our dynamic table
- Make the total sum of all the elements in the table.
- Being able to calculate sums or averages in business situations. For example, if you want to post a certain number of sales by department or region.
- To be able to sample the totals as a percentage of a whole. For example, compare the sales of a particular product with the total sales.
- Being able to generate lists that have unique values. For example, to show certain cities or countries that have requested or marketed a specific product.
- Creating a 2x2 table summary of a complex report.
- Easily identify the most frequent, average, maximum, and minimum values from a specific data set.
- Query information directly from an online analytical processing (OLAP) server.

Better manage our pivot tables with the PIVOT and UNPIVOT operators

The PIVOT and UNPIVOT relational operators offered by some tools, such as SQL servers, allow us to easily exchange rows' results by columns, called cross references.

Some database managers offer these operators, such as Oracle and SQL Server. Next, we will tell you the uses in sets of both operators and how they differ.

- Pivot

Using this operator in SQL Server, we can transform the rows returned by a query into single-value columns.

The syntax that must be carried out for the Pivot operator would be the following:

```
SELECT <<ColumnNames>>
FROM <<TableName>>
PIVOT
AggregateFunction(<<ColumnToBeAggregated>>)
FOR PivotColumn IN (<<PivotColumnValues>>)
) AS <<Alias>>
```

Next, we will see a practical example of where we can use this operator. The following data will be taken:

	Country	Year	Sales Amount
1	Austrailia	2005	1309047.1978
2	Austrailia	2007	3033784.2131
3	Austrailia	2006	2154284.8835
4	Austrailia	2008	2563884.29
5	Canada	2005	146829.8074
6	Canada	2008	673628.21
7	Canada	2006	621602.3823
8	Canada	2007	535784.4624
9	France	2007	1026324.9692
10	France	2005	180571.692
11	France	2008	922179.04
12	France	2006	514942.0131
13	Germany	2006	521230.8475
14	Germany	2007	1058405.7305
15	Germany	2005	237784.9902

The following data will be taken as input, and the pivot operator will be applied to it, as it was shown in the syntax of a few previous steps

```
SELECT FROM
PIVOT
[Country], [2005], [dbo]. [PivotExample]
[2006], [2007],
[2008]
SUM(SalesAmount)
FOR [Year] IN ([2005], [2006], [2007], [2008])
) AS P
```

The result that our query will return using the pivot operator will be the following:

	Country	Year	Sales Amount
1	Austrailia	2005	1309047.1978
2	Austrailia	2007	3033784.2131
3	Austrailia	2006	2154284.8835
4	Austrailia	2008	2563884.29
5	Canada	2005	146829.8074
6	Canada	2008	673628.21
7	Canada	2006	621602.3823
8	Canada	2007	535784.4624
9	France	2007	1026324.9692
10	France	2005	180571.692
11	France	2008	922179.04
12	France	2006	514942.0131
13	Germany	2006	521230.8475
14	Germany	2007	1058405.7305
15	Germany	2005	237784.9902

As we can see, grouping by years is done automatically since the grouping function (SUM) is being applied, and the unique values that correspond to the years are being used in the output as columns.

- Unpivot

To perform the opposite operation to what PIVOT does, that is, that the columns are transformed into rows, we use the SQL Server operator, UNPIVOT.

To better understand how the UNPIVOT operator works, we will use the following pivot table as input data, as shown:

Results		Messages			
	Country	2005	2006	2007	2008
1	Australia	1309047.1978	2154284.8835	3033784.2131	2563884.29
2	Canada	146829.8074	621602.3823	535784.4624	673628.21
3	France	180571.692	514942.0131	1026324.9692	922179.04
4	Germany	237784.9902	521230.8475	1058405.7305	1076890.77
5	UK	291590.5194	591586.854	1298248.5675	1210286.27
6	USA	1100549.4498	2126696.546	2838512.355	3324031.16

We will apply the same syntax as we did with the PIVOT operator; however, now we will apply UNPIVOT through the statement:

```
SELECT
Country, Year, SalesAmount
FROM [dbo]. [UnpivotExample]
UNPIVOT
(
SalesAmount
FOR [Year] IN ([2005], [2006], [2007], [2008])
) AS P
```

The results to be obtained in the table are the following:

Results		Messages	
	Country	Year	Sales Amount
1	Australia	2005	1309047.1978
2	Australia	2006	2154284.8835
3	Australia	2007	3033784.2131
4	Australia	2008	2563884.29
5	Canada	2005	146829.8074
6	Canada	2006	621602.3823
7	Canada	2007	535784.4624
8	Canada	2008	673628.21
9	France	2005	180571.692
10	France	2006	514942.0131
11	France	2007	1026324.9692
12	France	2008	922179.04
13	Germany	2005	237784.9902
14	Germany	2006	521230.8475
15	Germany	2007	1058405.7305

As we can see, it shows the data of our table by exchanging the columns and crossing the columns with the initial rows to obtain the complete table.

Chapter 8: Powerful Time Series Analysis

Let's talk about the distributed monitoring time series database.

A time series database is optimized for timestamp or time series data. Time series data means measurements or events that are tracked collected, or monitored over some time. This could be data collected from heartbeats from motion tracking sensors, JVM metrics from java applications, market trading data, network data, API responses, process uptime, etc.

Time series databases are fully customized with timestamped data, which is efficiently indexed and written in such a way that you can insert time series data. You can query that time series data much faster than you would in a relational environment or NoSQL Database.

InfluxDB

InfluxDB is a popular time series database among DevOps, written in Go. It was designed from the ground up to enable highly scalable data ingestion and storage while providing efficient ways to collect, store, query, visualize and take action on real-time time series data, events, and metrics. With InfluxDB, you can quickly analyze data streams, detect patterns and trends, and easily make informed decisions.

Provides resolution reduction and data retention policies to support keeping high-precision, high-value data in memory and lower-value data on disk. It is built cloud-native to provide scalability across multiple deployment topologies, including on-premises and hybrid cloud environments.

InfluxDB is an open-source and enterprise-ready solution. It uses InfluxQL, similar to a structure query language, to interact with the data. The latest version proposes agents, dashboards, queries, and tasks in one toolkit. It is an all-in-one tool for creating dashboards, visualizing, and alerting.

Features
- High performance for highly ingested time series data and real-time queries
- InfluxQL interacts with data as a query language
- The main component of the TICK stack (Telegraf, InfluxDB, Chronograf, and Kapacitor).
- Plugin support for protocols like collected, Graphite, and OpenTSDB for data ingestion
- It can handle millions of data points in just 1 second
- Retention policies to automatically delete out-of-date data

Since it is open source, you can download it and start it on your server. However, they offer InfluxDB Cloud on AWS, Azure, and GCP.

Prometheus

Prometeo is an open-source monitoring solution that provides insights from metrics data and sends necessary alerts. It uses a local time series database on disk to store data in a custom format, allowing for more flexibility and a more tailored approach to data collection.

The Prometheus data model is multidimensional and time series-based, so all data is stored as timestamped sequences of values. This is extremely helpful when working with numerical time series and collecting data from microservices. It lets you quickly query the data and obtain the necessary insights.

Features
- It has a multidimensional model that uses the name of the metrics and the key-value pairs (tags)
- PromQL to query time series data to generate Adhoc charts, alerts, and graphs
- Use HTTP pull mode to collect time series data
- Uses an intermediate gateway to push time series

Prometeo has hundreds of exporters to export your data from Windows, Linux, Java, Database, API, Website, Server Hardware, PHP, Messaging, and more.

TimescaleDB

TimelineDB is an open-source relational database that makes SQL scalable for time series data. This database is based on PostgreSQL.

Introducing TimescaleDB — the world's first open-source database designed for time-series data. Whether you need to monitor DevOps, track data from IoT devices, understand financial data, or measure logs, Kubernetes events, Prometheus metrics, and custom metrics, TimescaleDB has you covered.

It offers two products: For those looking to get up and running quickly, we offer two options: TimescaleDB Community Edition, free to use and install on your server, and TimescaleDB Cloud, a fully hosted and managed solution for your deployment needs. With TimescaleDB Community Edition, you get the same powerful database technology as TimescaleDB Cloud without infrastructure maintenance. With TimescaleDB Cloud, you get all the same features plus a fully managed and secure infrastructure in the cloud. Whatever your deployment needs, TimescaleDB has you covered.

For product owners, TimescaleDB can provide invaluable insights into your product's performance over time, helping you make strategic decisions for growth. Sign up today and experience the power of time-series data!

Features
- Run queries 10 to 100 times faster than PostgreSQL, MongoDB
- It can scale horizontally to petabytes of data and write millions of data points per second - making it a powerful solution for enterprise applications.
- Plus, it has a familiar PostgreSQL-like syntax, so it's easy for developers and administrators to operate.
- Combine functionalities of relational and time series databases to create powerful applications.
- Built-in algorithms and performance functions to save a lot of costs.

Graphite

Graphite is an all-in-one solution for efficiently storing and displaying real-time time series data. Graphite can do two things, store time series data and render graphs on demand. But it does not collect data; you can use tools like collected, Ganglia, Sensu, telegraph, etc.

It has three components: Carbon, Whisper, and Graphite Web. Carbon obtains the time series data, aggregates it, and perseveres it to disk. Whisper is a time series database store that stores the data. Graphite-Web is the front end for creating dashboards and visualizing the data.

Graphite characteristics:
- The metric format in which the data is submitted is simple.
- Comprehensive API to render data and create charts, dashboards, graphs
- Provides a rich set of transformative plotting functions and statistical Library
- Chain multiple render functions together to build a target query.

QuestDB

QuestDB is an advanced column-oriented relational database designed specifically for real-time analysis of time series data. Utilizing SQL and a few extensions to make a relational model for time series data, QuestDB has been expertly coded from the ground up with no dependencies, ensuring maximum performance. With the ability to perform relational and time series joins, QuestDB allows you to easily and quickly correlate data. To get started with QuestDB, deploy it inside a Docker container for the easiest and most convenient experience.

QuestDB Features:
Make data import and analytics easier with our interactive console! The console is compatible with cloud-native systems like AWS, Azure, and GCP, as well as on-premises and integrated systems. Plus, it provides enterprise integration with features like active directory, high availability, enterprise security, and clustering. Get real-time insights from operational and predictive analytics. Streamline data import and analytics today!

AWS Timestream

How can AWS not be on the list?
AWS Time Stream is a powerful, serverless time series database service that is fast, scalable, and cost-effective. It's optimized for ingesting, storing, and querying massive amounts of time series data, making it an ideal solution for IoT applications. With its specialized query engine, you can simultaneously query recent data and store historical data, allowing you to analyze time series data and uncover insights quickly. Plus, the built-in functions make getting the most out of your data even easier.

Amazon Timestream Features:

Streamline your data collection and analysis with our cloud-based service. Everything is taken care of automatically, with no servers to manage or instances to provision. Plus, the cost-effective pay-as-you-go model guarantees you only pay for what you consume, store, and view.

The platform can ingest trillions of events per day without sacrificing performance, and built-in analytics provide standard SQL, interpolation, and smoothing functions for quickly recognizing trends, patterns, and anomalies. Plus, all data is encrypted with the AWS Key Management System (KMS) and Customer Managed Keys (CMKs) for maximum security.

OpenTSDB

OpenTSDB is an incredibly powerful and scalable time series database built on HBase. It allows you to store an enormous amount of data points, with millions of writes per second, in a way that preserves their original timestamp and exact values so you don't lose any data.

To make this data storage and access even easier, OpenTSDB comes with a time series daemon (TSD) and command line utilities that make managing your data a breeze. You can communicate with the TSD via HTTP API, telnet, or its built-in GUI. Additionally, you can use tools such as Flume, Collected, and Vacuum Trim to collect data from different sources and import them into OpenTSDB.

OpenBSD Features:
- You can add, filter, and down resolution metrics at breakneck speed
- Stores and writes data with millisecond precision
- This powerful software runs on Apache Hadoop and HBase and can easily scale to accommodate larger workloads by adding additional nodes to the cluster. With this enhanced scalability, you can handle larger data sets and process more data in less time. Use GUI to generate graphs

Conclusion

As increasingly IoT/smart devices are being used these days, huge real-time traffic is being generated on websites with millions of events in a day, market trading is increasing, and the database of series of time has come. Time series databases are a must in your production stack for monitoring.

Most of the time series database mentioned above is available for self-hosting, so go ahead and get a cloud VM and try it to see what works for you.

Chapter 9: Cohort Analysis

Are you not getting enough insights from the data you have? It may be that you are observing them incorrectly. We recommend conducting a cohort or group analysis to obtain specific and meaningful information about your company and strategy.

Cohort analysis is an effective way to obtain actionable and unique data. The insights from this type of analysis can help companies achieve their marketing, sales, customer service goals, etc.

What is cohort analysis?

A cohort is a group of users or customers who share a set of characteristics during a specific period. Shared features can be:

- Customers who signed up during a specific month
- Customers who used your product before or after a specific launch
- Customers who, because of a specific marketing campaign, bought your product
- Customers using a specific feature in your app

- Your users depending on their level of purchase or use of your product
- The type of device your customers use to interact with you (phone app, website, etc.

How does cohort analysis work?

The cohort analysis or group analysis works like a behavior analysis. It focuses on observing customers to understand what they do, how they do it, and why they do it.

Cohort analysis makes it easier to see patterns throughout a customer's lifecycle. From this analysis, relevant and actionable information can be obtained that can be used in different specific stages of a customer's buying process.

Reviewing data from all your customers can help you gain useful insights and make comparisons of their actions or habits. Having these insights can help you to know what your customers do and why they do what they do and offer a better service as a company to generate more sales.

Based on the findings from this type of analysis, you can know how to create a positive experience or avoid repeating something negative in the process. Remember: Learning from customers helps you grow your business.

What should be analyzed?

When doing data analysis, you should do it to know how to meet your goals or initiatives. There is a lot of data that is worth following and studying. But you must know which data will produce the most positive and meaningful insights and results.

When deciding what data to track and study, keep the following questions in mind:

- What problem or question do you want to solve by studying this data specifically?
- What data will generate insights that can improve your current strategy?
- Will these insights help you meet your current business goals?

Who can benefit from cohort analysis?

They can be e-commerce companies, SaaS companies, marketing agencies, or companies looking to improve their user experience.

As a SaaS company, it can help you observe and improve how people interact with your product in its lifecycle. This will allow you to analyze your unique behavior retention, churn rates, and other vital metrics.

If you are an e-commerce company, it can be used to verify which of your marketing campaigns or promotions had a better impact and to understand what generates the most sales for you.

Cohort analysis helps companies calculate and improve the lifetime value of their customers. Knowing the lifetime value of your particular customers will also allow you to identify your most valuable customer segments and help you target your efforts in the right way to increase these value segments.

Understanding the lifetime value of your customers for specific groups will also help you determine how much you need to spend on acquiring and retaining these groups and maintaining profitability.

Cohort analysis is undoubtedly an analysis that helps marketers analyze and optimize specific campaigns and acquisition channels.

With the information obtained from this type of analysis, you can see which channels and campaigns produce better customers; with this in mind, you can spend more on high-performing channels or create similar campaigns. You can also optimize underperforming campaigns and channels in the hope that they will improve.

Cohort or group analysis will also help you answer questions like:

- When is the best time to engage with a user?
- How do your customers use your app?
- When is the good time to apply a "remarketing"?
- What behavior differences exist between users who logged in before and after a product release or update?
- What products attract the most customers to your website?
- Do these customers view and buy the products or view them?
- How much money does a customer spend on average?

Book 4: Advance SQL

Chapter 1: Advance SQL Value Expressions

SQL offers three ways to match text with a pattern: the traditional SQL statement, LIKE the more modern one (added in SQL:1999), and POSIX -style regular expressions. In addition to simple operators answering the question," does the string match this pattern?". PostgreSQL has functions to extract or replace matching substrings and to split a string according to a given pattern. SIMILAR TO

Clue

You can write your functions in Perl or Tcl if these built-in features are insufficient.

Attention

While most regular expression searches are very fast, regular expressions can be so complex that they can take a significant amount of time and memory to process. So beware of regular expression patterns coming from untrusted sources. If you have no choice, entering a timeout for operators is recommended.

Pattern matching SIMILAR TO carries the same security risks since the construct SIMILAR TO provides much of the same functionality as POSIX -style regular expressions.

Searching with LIKE is much easier than the other two options, so using it with untrusted search pattern sources is safer.

LIKE

stringLIKE [ESCAPE]

NOT LIKE [ESCAPE] pattern special character string pattern special character.

The expression LIKE returns true if it matches the given. (As you might expect, an expression returns false when it returns true, and vice versa. This expression is equivalent to expression .) pattern string NOT LIKE.

If it does not contain percent signs or underscores, then the pattern represents exactly a string and acts as a comparison operator. The underscore ( ) replaces (instead of it fits) any character, and the percent sign ( ) substitutes for any (including empty) sequence of characters.templateLIKE_template%

Here are a few examples:

'abc' LIKE 'abc'	true
'abc' LIKE 'a%'	true
'abc' LIKE '_b_'	true
'abc' LIKE 'c'	false

When checking against a pattern LIKE, the entire string is always considered. Therefore, if you want to find a sequence of characters somewhere in the middle of a string, the pattern must begin and end with percent signs.

You must add a special character before the corresponding character to find a literal occurrence of a percent sign or underscore in a string. The backslash is default selected as a special character, but you can choose another with a suggestion. To include a special character in your search pattern, duplicate it.templateESCAPE.

Note:

If the standard_conforming_strings option is disabled, each backslash character written in a text constant must be duplicated.

You can also opt-out of the special character by writing ESCAPE ''. In this case, the mechanism of special sequences is disabled, and it is impossible to use percent signs literally and underscores in the template.

LIKE The keyword can be used instead of ILIKE to make the search case-insensitive, considering the current language environment. This statement is not defined in the SQL standard; it's a PostgreSQL extension.

In addition, PostgreSQL has an operator ~~equivalent to LIKE, and ~~*corresponding to ILIKE. There are also two operators !~~and !~~*, representing NOT LIKE and NOT ILIKE, respectively. All of these operators are specific to PostgreSQL. You can see them, for example, in the output of the command EXPLAIN because when parsing the request, checks LIKE and the like are replaced by them.

The phrases LIKE, ILIKE, NOT LIKE, and in PostgreSQLNOT ILIKE syntax are usually treated as operators; for example, they can be used in ANY ( ) constructs, although a clause cannot be added here. In some special cases, it may still be necessary to use the underlying operators instead. Expression operatorsubexpressionESCAPE.

There is also a prefix check operator ^@and a corresponding function starts_withthat covers cases where you need to search only at the beginning of a string.

SIMILAR TO

Line SIMILAR TO [ESCAPE]

NOT SIMILAR TO [ESCAPE]

The operator SIMILAR TO returns true or false depending on whether the given string matches the pattern. It works like the LIKE, except that its patterns conform to the definition of regular expressions in the SQL standard. SQL regular expressions are an interesting syntactic hybrid LIKE with regular expression syntax.

Similarly, LIKE, the condition SIMILAR TO is true only if the pattern matches the entire string; this is different from regular expression conditions, where the pattern will match any part of the string, also, like LIKE, SIMILAR TO treats _and %as wildcards that substitute for any single character or any substring, respectively (in POSIX regular expressions, they are analogous to .and .*).

In addition to the template definitions borrowed from LIKE, it is SIMILAR TO support the following metacharacters inherited from POSIX regular expressions:

- | means a choice (one of two options).
- *means repeating the last element 0 or more times.
- +means repeating the last element one or more times.
- ?means the occurrence of the last element 0 or 1 time.
- {m}means repeating the last element exactly once.m
- {m,}means repeating the last element or more times.m
- {m,n}means repeating the previous element at least and at most times.mn
- Parentheses ()combine multiple elements into one logical group.
- Square brackets [...]designate a character class in the same way as in POSIX regular expressions.

Note that the dot (.) is not a metacharacter for the operator SIMILAR TO.

As with LIKE, the backslash overrides the special meaning of any of these metacharacters, and the clause ESCAPE allows another special character to be chosen.

Here are a few examples:

'abc' SIMILAR TO 'abc'   true

'abc' SIMILAR TO 'a'   false

'abc' SIMILAR TO '%(b|d)%' true

'abc' SIMILAR TO '(b|c)%'   false

TO"

A function substring with three parameters extracts a substring that matches an SQL regular expression pattern. As with, the entire string must match the specified pattern; otherwise, the function will find nothing and return NULL. To indicate the part of the template that should be returned on success, the template must contain two special characters and quotes ( ) after each. This function returns the part of the pattern between two such markers. Substring SIMILAR TO"

Some examples with markers #" highlighting the returned string:

```
substring('foobar' from '%#"o_b#"%' for '#')    oob
substring('foobar' from '#"o_b#"%' for '#')     NULL
```

POSIX

Regular expression operators

operator	Description	example
~	Checks if a regular expression matches a case sensitive	'Thomas' ~ '.*thomas.*'
~*	Matches a regular expression in a case-insensitive manner	'Thomas' ~* '.*Thomas.*'
!~	Checks if a regular expression does not match, case sensitive	'Thomas' !~ '.*Thomas.*'
!~*	Checks if a regular expression does not match, case insensitive	'thomas' !~* '.*vadim.*'

POSIX regular expressions provide more powerful pattern-matching capabilities than the LIKE and operators SIMILAR TO. Many Unix commands, such as egrep, use seda awktemplating language similar to the one described here.

A regular expression is a sequence of characters that is a shorthand definition for a set of strings (a standard set). A string is considered to match a regular expression if it is a member of the regular set described by the regular expression. As with LIKE, wildcard characters directly match characters in the string, except special regular expression language characters. At the same time, special characters in regular expressions differ from special characters LIKE. Unlike patterns LIKE, a regular expression can match any part of a string unless it is explicitly tied to the beginning and end of the string.

Here are a few examples:

```
'abc' ~ 'abc'     true
'abc' ~ '^a'      true
'abc' ~ '(b|d)'   true
'abc' ~ '^(b|c)'  false
```

The POSIX -style templating language is described in more detail below.

The function substring with two parameters extracts a substring which matches a POSIX regular expression pattern. It returns a text that matches the pattern if there is one in the string or NULL otherwise. But if the pattern contains parentheses, it returns the first parenthesized subexpression (the one that starts with the first opening parenthesis). If you want to use parentheses but not in this special mode, you can enclose the entire expression in parentheses. If you need to include parentheses in the pattern before the subexpression you want to extract, you can do so using non-capturing groups.

Here are a few examples:

```
substring('foobar' from 'ob')      oob
substring('foobar' from 'o(.)b')   o
```

fragment.

The function regexp_replacesubstitutes other text for substrings matching POSIX regular expression patterns. It has the syntax regexp_replace(, [,]). If it does not contain a fragment matching the, it is returned unchanged. If a match is found, it returns, which is substituted for the corresponding fragment.

Here are a few examples:

```
regexp_replace('foobarbaz', 'b..', 'X')
fooXbaz
regexp_replace('foobarbaz', 'b..', 'X', 'g')
fooXX
regexp_replace('foobarbaz', 'b(..)', 'X\1Y', 'g')
fooXarYXazY
```

The function regexp_matchreturns a text array of all matching substrings obtained from the first occurrence of the POSIX regular expression pattern in the string. It has the syntax regexp_match(, [,]). If the entry is not found, the result is. If the occurrence is found and does not contain parenthesized subexpressions, the result is a text array with one element containing the substring that matches the entire pattern. If an occurrence is found and contains parenthesized subexpressions, the result is a text array in which the -th element is the -th parenthesized subexpression (not counting "non-capturing. " In the parameter, an optional text string is passed, containing zero or more one-letter flags that change the function's behavior. Valid flags are described in Table.

Some examples:

```
SELECT regexp_match('foobarbequebaz', 'bar.*que');
 regexp_match
 -------------
 {barbeque}
 (1 row)
SELECT regexp_match('foobarbequebaz', '(bar)(beque)');
 regexp_match
 -------------
 {bar,beque}
 (1 row)
```

In general, you can get the entire found substring or NULLif there is no match, you can do something like this:

```
SELECT (regexp_match('foobarbequebaz', 'bar.*que'))[1];
 regexp_match
 -------------
 barbeque
 (1 row)
```

The function regexp_matchesreturns a set of text arrays with all matching substrings resulting from applying a POSIX regular expression to the string. It has the same syntax as regexp_match. This function does not return any rows if there are no matches; it returns one string if one occurrence is found and no flag is passed g, or rows if matches are found, and the flag is passed. Each returned string is a text array containing all the found substrings or substrings matching the parenthesized subexpressions, as described above.

Here are a few examples:

```
SELECT regexp_matches('foo', 'not there');
 regexp_matches
 ----------------
 (0 rows)
SELECT regexp_matches('foobarbequebazilbarfbonk', '(b[^b]+)(b[^b]+)', 'g');
 regexp_matches
 ----------------
 {bar,beque}
 {basil,barf}
 (2 rows
```

Clue:

regexp_matches()Should be used with the flag in most cases g because if you're only interested in the first occurrence, it's easier and more efficient to use the regexp_match(). Nevertheless, regexp_match()only exists in PostgreSQL version 10 and above. Older versions usually put the call regexp_matches()in a nested SELECT, like this:

```
SELECT col1, (SELECT regexp_matches(col2, '(bar)(beque)')) FROM tab;
```

The result is a text array if the match is found or NULL; otherwise, just like with regexp_match(). Without a nested SELECT, this query doesn't return any rows if no match is found, which is usually not what you want.

The function regexp_split_to_tablesplits the string using a POSIX regular expression pattern as the delimiter. It contains the syntax regexp_split_to_table(, [,]). If not in the passed string, the entire string is returned. If at least one occurrence is found, for each such occurrence, the text from the end of the previous occurrence (or the beginning of the line) to the beginning of the occurrence is returned. After the last occurrence is found, the fragment is returned from its end to the end of the string. The optional parameter is a text string containing zero or more one-letter flags that change the function's behavior. The flags supported are described in Table.

The function regexp_split_to_arraybehaves like regexp_split_to_table, except that it regexp_split_to_arrayreturns the result in an array of elements of type text. It contains the syntax regexp_split_to_array(, [,]).

Here are a few examples:

```
SELECT foo FROM regexp_split_to_table('the quick brown fox jumps over the lazy dog', '\s+') AS foo;
 foo
-------
 the
 quick
 brown
 Fox
 jumps
 over
 the
 lazy
 dog
(9 rows)
SELECT regexp_split_to_array('the quick brown fox jumps over the lazy dog', '\s+');
        regexp_split_to_array
--------------------------------------------
```

```
{the,quick,brown,fox,jumps,over,the,lazy,dog}
(1 row)
SELECT foo FROM regexp_split_to_table('the quick brown fox', '\s*') AS foo;
 foo
-----
 t
 h
 e
 q
 u
 i
 c
 k
 b
 r
 o
 w
 n
 f
 o
 x
(16 rows)
```

As the last example shows, regular expression splitting functions ignore zero-length occurrences at the beginning and end of the string and immediately after the previous occurrence. This behavior is contrary to the strict definition of regular expression matching that the regexp_matchand functions implement regexp_matches, but is usually more convenient in practice. Similar behavior is observed in other programming environments, such as Perl.

A detailed description of regular expressions

Regular expressions in PostgreSQL are implemented using a software package developed by Henry Spencer. Almost all the following regular expressions descriptions are copied verbatim from his manual.

A regular expression (RE), as defined in POSIX, can take two forms: an extended RE or ERE (roughly speaking, these are expressions that egrep) and a simple RE or BRE (roughly speaking, these are expressions for ed). PostgreSQL supports both forms and implements some extensions not provided by the POSIX standard but are widely used due to their availability in some programming languages, such as Perl and Tcl. Regular expressions using these non-POSIX-compliant extensions are enhanced REs .or ARE. AREs are practically a superset of EREs, while BREs have some notational inconsistencies (besides being much more limited). We first describe the forms of ARE and ERE, noting the features unique to ARE, and then we will tell you how BRE differs from them.

Note:

PostgreSQL always assumes by default that a regular expression follows the ARE rules. However, you can switch to the more restrictive ERE or BRE rules by adding the built-in parameter to the RE template. This is useful for compatibility with applications that expect the DBMS to follow the POSIX rules strictly.

A regular expression is declared as one or more branches separated by |. It is considered to correspond to everything that corresponds to one of these branches.

A branch is zero or more quantitative atoms or constraints connected. A branch match is formed from a first-part match, followed by a second-part match, and so on; a bare branch matches an empty string.

A quantitative atom is an atom that a quantifier can follow. Without this determinant, it corresponds to one occurrence of an atom. With a quantifier, it can correspond to some number of occurrences of that atom.

The constraint matches the empty string, but this match is only possible if certain conditions are met. Constraints can be used the same way as atoms, except that they cannot be supplemented with quantifiers. Simple limits are shown below; some additional restrictions are described below.

Regular expression atoms

Atom	Description
(re)	(where is any regular expression) describes a match, while this match is captured for further processing re re
(?:re)	like the previous one, but the match is not captured (i.e., it is a set of " no capturing " brackets) (only applies to ARE)
.	matches any character
[symbol]	expression in square brackets
\k	(where is not an alphanumeric character) matches a regular character, i.e., matches a backslash k \ \
\c	where is an alphanumeric character (which may be followed by other characters), this is a special character, (only applies to ARE; in ERE and BRE, this atom corresponds to)c
{	When this character is followed by any character other than a digit, this atom matches a left curly brace ({); if a digit follows it, it marks the start.
x	(where is a single character with no special meaning) matches that character x

The RE expression cannot end with a backslash (\).

Note:

If the standard_conforming_strings option is disabled, each backslash character written in a text constant must be duplicated.

Determinant	Corresponds
*	0 or more occurrences of an atom
+	One or more occurrences of an atom
?	0 or 1 atom occurrences
{m}	exactly occurrences of an atom m
{m,}	m or more occurrences of an atom
{m,n}	from to (including boundaries)

	occurrences of an atom; can't be moremnmn
*?	not a greedy version*
+?	not a greedy version+
??	Not a greedy version?
{m}?	not a greedy version{m}
{m,}?	not a greedy version{m,}
{m,n}?	not a greedy version{m,n}

Quantifiers in regular expressions

In forms with numbers and define the so-called quantity limits. These numbers must be unsigned decimal integers between 0 and 255 inclusive. {...}mn

Non-greedy qualifiers (allowed only in ARE) describe the same possible matches as their regular counterparts (" greedy ") but prefer to choose the fewest rather than the most occurrences.

Note:

Quantifiers cannot follow one after the other; for example, the entry **will be erroneous. In addition, specifiers cannot appear at the beginning of an expression or subexpression and immediately after ^or |.

Restrictions in regular expressions

Limitation	Description
^	matches the beginning of the string
$	matches the end of the string
(?=re)	positive lookahead finds a match where the matching substring begins (ARE only), re
(?!re)	negative lookahead finds a match where the matching substring does not start (ARE only), re
(?<=re)	positive look back finds a match where the matching substring ends (ARE only)re
(?<!re)	negative lookback finds a match where the matching substring does not end (ARE only)re

Forward and backward lookup constraints cannot contain backlinks, and all parentheses are considered "non-capturing parentheses."

Expressions in square brackets

The expression in square brackets contains a list of characters enclosed in []. Usually, it matches any character from the list (the exception is described below). If the list begins with ^, it matches any character not listed later in the list. If two characters are separated by -in the list, this is taken as shorthand for the full range of characters between (and including) the two given ones in the sort order; for example, an ASCII expression [0-9]matches any decimal digit. Two intervals cannot share the same boundary, i.e., the expression is a-c-invalid. The intervals depend on the sort order, which can change, so it is better not to use them in portable programs.

To be included in the list], this character must be written first (immediately after ^if present). Including a character in the list must be written first, last, or as the second boundary of the interval. You can specify -an interval as the first boundary by enclosing it between [.and .]so that it becomes the sort element (see below) except for these characters, some combinations of c [(see the following paragraphs) and special characters (in ARE), all other special characters in square brackets lose their special meaning. In particular, an \ERE or BRE character is treated as normal, although it escapes the character that follows it in ARE.

Expressions in square brackets can contain a sort element (a character or sequence of characters, or the name of such a sequence) whose definition is between [.and .]. The sequence defining it is perceived in the expression in brackets as one element. This allows such expressions to include elements corresponding to a sequence of multiple characters. For example, with a sort element chin square brackets, the regular expression [[.ch.]]*cwill match the first five characters of the string chchcc.

Note:

PostgreSQL does not currently support multi-character sort items. This information refers to possible future behavior.

The square brackets can contain collation elements between [=and =]denoting equivalence classes, i.e., sequences of characters from all sorting elements that are equivalent to the specified one, including itself. (If there is no equivalent for that character, it is treated as enclosed between [.and .].) For example, if eand ëare members of the same equivalence class, the expressions [[=e=]], [[=ë=]], and [eë]will be equivalent. An equivalence class cannot be specified as the boundary of an interval.

The square brackets can also contain the name of a character class enclosed between [: and :], replacing the list of all characters in that class. Common class names: alnum, alpha, blank, cntrl, digit, graph, lower, print, punct, space, and xdigit. This whole set of classes is defined in ctype and can change depending on the locale (language environment). A character class cannot be used as a range boundary either.

There are two special kinds of square bracket expressions: expressions [[:<:]]and [[:>:]], which are constraints that match empty strings at the beginning and end of a word. A word in this context is defined as a sequence of word-component characters before or after which there are no word-component characters. A word character is either a class character alnum(defined in ctype) or an underscore. This extension is POSIX compliant but not defined there and should therefore be used cautiously where compatibility with other systems is important. It's usually better to use the delimiting special characters described below; they are also not quite standard but easier to type.

Regular expression special characters

Special characters are special commands consisting of \followed by an alphanumeric character. The categories of special characters can be distinguished: character designs, class codes, restrictions, and back links. A character \followed by an alphanumeric character that does not form a valid special character is considered an error in ARE. There are no special characters in ERE: outside of square brackets, a pair of from \and the following alphanumeric character is perceived simply as a given character, and in square brackets, the character itself is \perceived simply as a backslash. (The latter breaks the compatibility between ERE and ARE.)

Symbol special notations are introduced to facilitate the introduction of non-printable and other inconvenient characters into RE.

Class codes are shorthand for the names of some common character classes.

Restriction special characters denote restrictions that, if certain conditions match, are matched by an empty string.

The back reference ( ) matches the same string as the previous parenthesized subexpression at number. For example, ([bc])\1matches bbor ccbut not bcor cb. This subexpression must completely precede the back reference in the RE. Subexpressions are numbered in the order of their opening brackets. In this case, parentheses without capturing are excluded from consideration.

Special characters in regular expressions

special character	Description
\a	bell symbol, as in C
\b	backspace character, as in C
\B	synonym for backslash (\), reducing the need for duplication of this character
\cX	(where is any character) a character whose lower 5 bits are the same as y and the rest are 0XX
\e	the character specified in the sort sequence named ESC, or, if none is specified, the character with an octal value033
\f	form submission like in C
\n	newline like in C
\r	carriage return as in C

\t	horizontal tab like in C
\uwxyz	(where exactly four hexadecimal digits) a character with hexadecimal codewxyz0xwxyz
\Ustuvwxyz	(where exactly eight hexadecimal digits) a character with hexadecimal codestuvwxyz0xstuvwxyz
\v	vertical tab like in C
\xhhh	(where - multiple hexadecimal digits) a character with hexadecimal code (the character is always the same regardless of the number of hexadecimal digits)hhh0xhhh
\0	character with code 0(zero byte)
\xy	(where are exactly two octal digits, no back reference) a character with octal codexy0xy
\xyz	(where are exactly three octal digits, not a backlink) a character with octal codexyz0xyz

Hexadecimal digits are written 0as - 9 and a- for A- F. Octal digits are from 0 to 7.

Special sequences with numeric codes that specify values outside the ASCII range (0-127) are perceived differently depending on the database encoding. When the database is UTF-8 encoded, the special Code is the same as the character's position in Unicode, e.g., \u1234the character U+1234. For other multi-byte encodings, special sequences are usually just a series of bytes that define the character. If the character specified by the special sequence is missing in the database encoding, there will be no error, but no data will match it.

Characters passed by special notation are always treated as normal characters. For example, \135encodes]in ASCII, the special sequence \135will not close the expression in square brackets.

Class special codes in regular expressions

special character	Description
\d	[[:digit:]]
\s	[[:space:]]
\w	[[:alnum:]_](underlining also included)
\D	[^[:digit:]]
\S	[^[:space:]]
\W	[^[:alnum:]_](underlining also included

In bracketed expressions, the special characters \d, \sand \wlose their outer square brackets, while \D, \Sand \Ware is not allowed. (So, for example, the entry is [a-c\d]equivalent to [a-c[: digit:]]. And the entry [a-c\D], which would be equivalent to [a-c^[: digit:]], is invalid.)

Restriction of special characters in regular expressions

special character	Description
\A	matches only the beginning of the string (how this differs from ^)
\m	matches only the beginning of a word
\M	matches only the end of a word
\y	matches only the beginning or end of a word
\Y	matches only the position, not at the beginning and not at the end of the word
\Z	matches only the end of the string (how this differs from $)

The definition of the word here is the same as that given above in the description [[:<:]]and [[:>:]]. Restriction special characters are not allowed in square brackets.

backlinks in regular expressions

, special character	Description
\m	(where is a digit other than 0) is a link back to the subexpression under the numbermm
\mnn	(where is a digit other than 0, and is a few more digits with a decimal value not exceeding the number of capturing parentheses closed so far) reference back to subexpression numbermnnmnnmnn

Note:

Regular expressions have an inherent ambiguity between octal character codes and backlinks, resolved as follows (as mentioned above). A leading zero is always considered a sign of an octal sequence. A single digit other than 0 that is not followed by another digit is always treated as a backlink. A sequence of multiple digits that does not begin with 0 is treated as a backreference if it follows a matching subexpression (i.e., the number is in the range allowed for a backreference). Otherwise, it is treated as an octal number.

Regular expression metasyntax

In addition to the basic syntax described above, several special forms and various syntactic conveniences can also be used.

A regular expression can start with one of two special mode prefixes. If RE starts with ***: its continuation is treated as ARE. (In PostgreSQL, this usually doesn't matter since regular expressions are treated as ARE by default; but it can be useful when the regex function parameter includes ERE or BRE mode.)

ARE can start with built-in options: a sequence (where is one or more alphanumeric characters) that specifies the options for the rest of the regular expression. These options override any previously defined options; in particular, they can override the case-sensitivity mode implied by the regex operator or a regex function parameter. Valid parameter letters are shown in the Table below. Note that the same letters are used in the regex function parameter.

ARE Built-in Parameter Letters

Parameter	Description
b	regular expression continuation - BRE
c	match case sensitive (overrides operator type)
e	continuation of RE-ERE
i	match case-insensitively (overrides operator type)
m	historical synonym.n
n	Search for matches taking into account newlines
p	newlines are partially accounted for
q	the continuation of the regular expression is a regular string (" in quotes "), the contents of which are taken literally
s	Search for matches without taking into account newlines (default)
t	compact syntax (default; see below)
w	newlines are partially taken into account but in a different, " weird " mode.
x	extended syntax (see below)

Embedded options take effect immediately after the parenthesis)that terminates their sequence. They can only appear at the beginning of an ARE (after the ***: if present).

In addition to the regular (compact) RE syntax, in which all characters matter, an expanded syntax is also supported, which can be enabled using the built-in parameter x. The expanded syntax ignores whitespace characters and all characters from #up to the end of the string (or the end of the RE). This allows you to split the RE into lines and add comments. But there are three exceptions:

- A whitespace character or #, followed by \, is preserved
- a whitespace character or #within an expression in square brackets preserved
- whitespace characters, and comments cannot be present in compound characters, for example, in(?:

In this context, whitespace characters are spaces, tabs, newlines, and any other character that belongs to the character class .space

Finally, in ARE, a sequence (where is any text that does not contain) outside square brackets is also considered a comment and is completely ignored. However, it also cannot be inside compound characters such as. These commentaries are more of a historical legacy than a useful tool; they are considered deprecated, and it is recommended to use the extended syntax instead.

None of these metasyntax extensions will work if the expression begins with the prefix***=after, which takes the string literally and not as RE.

Regular Expression Matching Rules

When an RE can match more than one substring in a given string, the matching RE is the substring that begins in it first. If there are several similar corresponding substrings to a given position, the longest or the shortest possible substring is selected, depending on which mode is selected in RE: greedy or not greedy.

Where the following rules determine the greedy or non-greedy nature of the RE:

- Most atoms and all constraints do not have the greed flag (because they still cannot match substrings of different compositions).
- The parentheses surrounding the RE do not affect its "greed."
- An atom with a fixed quantity determinant (or) has the same greed characteristic (or may not have it) as the atom itself. {m} {m}?
- An atom with other normal quantifiers (including where equals) is considered greedy (prefers a full-length match). {m,n} mn
- An atom with a non-greedy quantifier (including, where equals) is considered non-greedy (prefers a minimum length match). {m,n}? mn
- A branch (RE with no top-level operator |) has the same greed characteristic as the first number atom in it that has the greedy attribute.
- An RE formed from two or more branches connected by the operator | is always considered greedy.

These rules associate greed characteristics with individual quantitative atoms and branches and whole REs containing quantitative atoms. When matched, a branch or integer RE can match the longest or shortest substring in the whole. When the length of the entire match is determined, the part corresponding to a particular subexpression is determined, taking into account the greedy characteristic for that subexpression, with subexpressions beginning earlier in RE taking precedence than those following them.

The following example illustrates this:

```
SELECT SUBSTRING('XY1234Z', 'Y*([0-9]{1,3})');
result:123
SELECT SUBSTRING('XY1234Z', 'Y*?([0-9]{1,3})');
result:1
```

In the first case, RE is generally greedy since the atom is greedy Y*. Its match starts with a letter Yand includes the maximum length substring from that point on, i.e., the substring Y123. The result of an expression is its part corresponding to the subexpression in brackets, i.e., 123. In the second case, the RE as a whole inherits the non-greedy character from the atom Y*?. Its match also starts with Y, but it includes the substring of the minimum length from this point on, i.e., Y1. And although [0-9]{1,3}the subexpression is greedy, it cannot affect the choice of the length of the match as a whole, so it remains only the substring 1.

In other words, when a RE contains both greedy and non-greedy subexpressions, the entire match will be as long or short as possible, depending on the characteristics of the entire RE. The characteristics associated with subexpressions only affect how much of a substring one subexpression can " absorb " relative to another.

To explicitly characterize a subexpression or an entire RE as "greedy" or "non-greedy," the qualifiers {1,1}and {1,1}? Respectively, it can be used. This is useful when you want the overall greed characteristic of an RE to be different from that implied by its elements. For example, suppose you are trying to extract from a string containing multiple digits those digits and the parts before and after them. You can try to do it like this:

```
SELECT regexp_match('abc01234xyz', '(.*)(\d+)(.*)');
result:{abc0123,4,xyz}
```

But this will not work: the first group .*is "greedy"; it will " eat " everything it can, leaving \d+only the last opportunity to match, that is, the last digit. You can try to make the request "non-greedy":

SELECT regexp_match('abc01234xyz', '(.*?)(\d+)(.*)');
result:{abc,0,""}

And that won't work, so now the entire RE has become non-greedy, and all matches are completed as soon as possible. But we can get the result we want by explicitly making everything RE greedy:

SELECT regexp_match('abc01234xyz', '(?:(.*?)(\d+)(.*)){1,1}');
result:{abc,01234,xyz}

Controlling an RE's overall greediness, regardless of its components' greediness, gives more flexibility in describing variable length patterns.

When specifying a longer or shorter match, the lengths of the matches are specified in characters, not in sort elements. An empty string is considered longer than no match. For example, an expression bb*matches three characters in the middle of a string abbbc, an expression matches (week|wee)(night|knights)all ten characters weeknights; when the expression is (.*).*matched against the string abc, the parenthesized subexpression matches all three characters; and when (a*)*matched against the string bc, both the RE as a whole and the parenthesized substring match the empty string.

Ignoring the case of characters gives almost the same effect as if the distinction between uppercase and lowercase letters in the alphabet disappeared. Suppose a letter in both uppercase and lowercase appears outside the square brackets as a normal character. In that case, it is effectively converted to a bracketed expression containing both, such as xas [xX]. If it appears in the expression in square brackets, all its variants are added to this expression; for example, [x] becomes [xX], and [^x]- [^xX].

When linefeed accounting mode is enabled, the atom .and expressions in square brackets with ^will never match end-of-line characters (so matches will never cross line boundaries if there are no explicit references to these characters in RE), ^and $will match an empty substring, not only at the beginning and end of the entire text but also at the beginning and end of each line. However, the special characters ARE \Aand \Zwill still match only the beginning and end of the entire text.

In the mode where newlines are partially taken into account, newlines have special meaning for atom .and expressions in square brackets, but not for ^and $.

In reverse partial mode, newlines have special meaning for ^and $, as in newline-sensitive mode, but not for .bracketed expressions. This mode is not very useful but exists for symmetry.

Limits and Compatibility

The current implementation lacks any explicit limit on the length of a RE. However, when developing highly portable programs, you should not use REs longer than 256 bytes, as another POSIX-compliant implementation may refuse to handle such regular expressions.

The only feature of ARE that is truly incompatible with the POSIX ERE is that in ARE, the character \does not lose its special meaning in square brackets. All other ARE extensions use syntax features that are not defined, allowed, or supported by the ERE; the mode switch syntax (***) is outside the POSIX syntax for both BRE and ERE.

Many ARE extensions are borrowed from the Perl language, but some have been changed, optimized, and a few Perl extensions have been dropped. As a result, the following incompatibilities occur in atoms \band \B, no special handling of trailing newlines, the addition of square bracket exceptions in the number of cases where newlines are taken into account, special conditions for parentheses and backlinks in lookahead/backward constraints, and " longest/" semantics. Short match " (instead of " first match ").

It is important to note two incompatibilities between ARE syntax and ERE regular expressions that PostgreSQL accepted before the version:

- In ARE \, followed by an alphanumeric character represents either a special character or an erroneous sequence, while in previous versions, it was possible to write alphanumeric characters this way. This shouldn't be a big problem since there was no reason to use such sequences.

- In ARE, the character \retains its special meaning in [], so to \be written literally in square brackets, it must be written as \\.

Simple regular expressions

BREs have several differences from EREs. In BRE, the characters |, +and ?lose their special meaning, and there is no replacement for them. Quantity bounds are surrounded by symbols \{and \}, while {and }are treated as normal symbols. Nested subexpressions are placed between \(and \), and (and)represent normal characters. A character ^is treated as a regular character unless it is at the beginning of a RE or a parenthesized subexpression, $is also a recurring character unless it is at the end of a RE or the end of a parenthesized subexpression, and*is a recurring character when it is at the beginning of a RE or a subexpression in parentheses (perhaps after the initial ^). And finally, backlinks with one digit work in BRE, \<and\>are synonyms for [[:<:]]and [[:>:]], respectively; no other special characters are supported in BRE.

Chapter 2: Relational Operators

Relational operators are symbols used to compare two values. If the comparison result is correct, the considered expression is true. Otherwise, it is false.

The comparison, 8>4 (eight greater than four), is true and is represented by the value 1, whereas 8<4 (eight less than four) is false and is represented by the value 0. In the first column of the Table, the symbols of the relational operators are given, and in the second, the name of said operators and their meaning utilizing an example.

Operator	Name	Example	Meaning
<	smaller than	a<b	a is less than b
>	greater than	a>b	a is greater than b
==	equal to	a==b	a is equal to b
~=	not equal to	a~=b	a is not equal to b
<=	less than or equal to	a<=5	a is less than or equal to b
>=	greater than or equal to	a>=b	a is less than or equal to b

MATLAB does not have the boolean data type (true, false); if the expression is true, it gives the result 1; if it is false, it gives the result 0.

```
>> 5>4
ans = 1
```
The ~ character is obtained by holding the Alt key and pressing the 126 keys on the numeric keypad. It corresponds to the ASCII decimal character 126.

```
>> 5>6
ans = 0
```
Special care must be taken not to confuse the assignment operator with the relational operator equal to. Assignments are made with the symbol =, and comparisons with ==.

If two scalars a Y b are compared, the result can be true (1) or false (0) according to the Table above.

Yes, a Y b are vectors of the same dimension, and each element is compared ai) with bi). The result is that the element (Yo) of the result vector u(i) can contain a 1 or 0.

Suppose two matrices (of the same dimensions) are compared. In that case, the comparison is made element by element, and the result is another matrix of the same dimension with ones and zeros according to the comparison result.

```
>> a=[15 6 9 4 11 7 14]
a= 15 6 9 4 11 7 14
>> b=[8 20 9 2 19 7 10]
b= 8 20 9 2 19 7 10
>> u=a>=b
u =
   1 0 1 1 0 1 1
```

A vector or matrix-like or containing ones and zeros is a special type of vector or matrix called logical and is widely used in MATLAB, as we will see on this page.

logical operators

- & AND (result is true if both expressions are true)
- | OR (result is true if any expression is true)

- ~ NOT (result reverses the condition of the expression)

AND and OR work with two operands and return a logical value based on so-called truth tables. The NOT operator acts on an operand. These truth tables are known and used in the context of daily life, for example: "if it is sunny AND I have time, I will go to the beach," "if it is NOT sunny, I will stay at home," "if it rains OR it is wind, I'll go to the movies." The truth tables of the AND, OR, and NOT operators are shown in the following tables.

The logical operator AND, &

x	Y	Outcome
1	1	1
1	0	0
0	1	0
0	0	0

The logical operator OR,

x	Y	Outcome
1	1	1
1	0	1
0	1	1
0	0	0

| The logical operator NOT, ~

x	Outcome
1	0
0	1

The AND and OR operators combine relational expressions whose result is given by the last column of their truth tables. For example:

(a<b) & (b<c)

is true if both are true. If either or both are false, the result is false. Instead, the expression

(a<b) | (b<c)

It is true if one of the two comparisons is true. If both are false, the result is false. The expression "NOT a is less than b."

~(a<b)

is false if (a<b) is true and is true if the comparison is false. Therefore, the NOT operator changes the state from true to false and from false to true.

MATLAB has functions that are equivalent to logical operators. These are:

and(x,y) equivalent to, x&y

or(x,y) equivalent to, x|y

not(x) equivalent to, ~x

Logical operators, in combination with relational ones, can also be applied to vectors,

```
>> a=[1 5 3 7];
>> b=[0 2 8 7];
>> u=(a>b) & (a>4)
u=
  0 1 0 0
>> u=(a>b) | (a>4)
u=
  1 1 0 1
```

```
>> a=[15 6 9 4 11 7 14]
a= 15   6 9 4   11   7   14
>> u=a<10
u = 0   1 1 1   0   1   0
>> c=a(u)
c =
  6 9 4 7
```

Access to the elements of a vector

We have already studied how to access the elements of a vector or a matrix through their indices; on this page, we will see new ways to access these elements when they meet certain conditions. To get the elements of the vector a that is less than 10

The vector u=a<10 contains ones and zeros due by comparing each element of vector a with 10. If it is less, it returns one. If it is greater than or equal, it returns 0. However, c=a(u) creates a vector consisting of those elements of the vector a, which correspond to 1 in the vector or.

be the vector x=[-4,0,5,-3,0,3,7,-1,6]; , we are going to count how many elements of the vector x are positive, negative or null

```
>> x=[-4,0,5,-3,0,3,7,-1,6]
x = -4 0 5 -3 0 3 7 -1 6
>> u=x<0
u = 1 0 0 1 0 0 0 1 0
>> ne=sum(u)
ne = 3
>> pos=sum(x>0)
pos = 4
>> zero=sum(x==0)
zero = 2
```

Product of a vector by a logical vector

We are going to calculate the element-by-element product of the vector a by the logical vector, which we will use in the following sections

```
>> a=[15,6,9,4,11,7,14]
a = 15 6 9 4 11 7 14
>> u =[0,1,1,1,0,1,0]
u = 0 1 1 1 0 1 0
>> a.u
ans =
    0 6 9 4 0 7 0
```

Represent the positive part of a function

Represent the function f (x) defined as follows

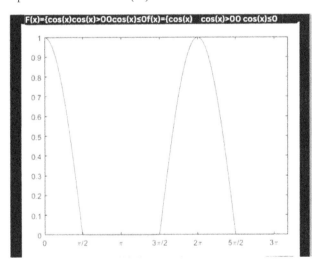

The expression y>0 returns a vector whose elements are 1 when cos(x) is positive and 0 otherwise. item-by-item product y.*(y>0) keeps the positive values unchanged and makes the others zero.

Represent a step function

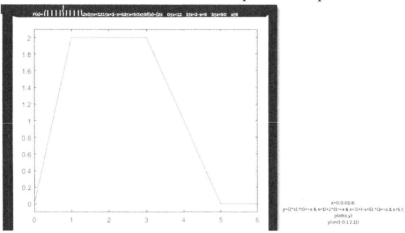

Avoiding division by zero

Suppose we need to graph the function y =sin(x)/ x from -4π to 4π. But when x is zero, we have a division by zero. To avoid this problem is to replace x =0 with x=eps. If we write eps in the command window, we get a very small number, 2.2204e-016.

The expression x==0 returns a one when x=0, then x takes the final value x=eps, which prevents division by 0.

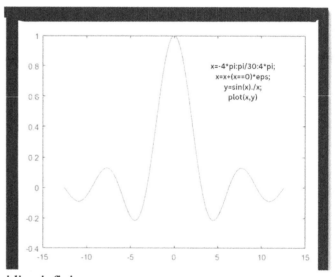

Avoiding infinity

Let's draw the function y =tan(x) from -3π/2 to 3π/2. The problem is that tan (x) approaches ±∞ when x =±π/2, ±3π/2,

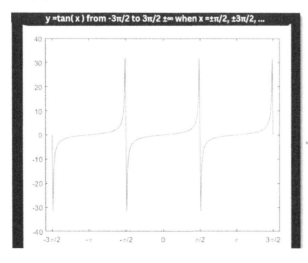

Abs (y)<100 returns a vector that is zero only near the asymptotes (when the tangent is very large in absolute value) and a one otherwise. It is suggested to put a comment symbol % in front of the

third line to override it, save the script, and test the effect.

MATLAB functions

xor(a,b)	exclusive OR. Returns 1 if one operand is true and the other is false. Returns 0 if both are true or both are false.	>> xor(7,0) ans = 1 >> xor(7,-5) ans = 0
there)	Returns 1 if all elements of the vector are nonzero. Returns 0 if one or more elements are zero	>>a = [5 3 11 7 8 15]; >> there ans =1 >> b = [3 6 11 4 0 13]; >> all(b) ans = 0
any(a)	Returns 1 if there are elements of the vector that are nonzero. If all the elements of the vector are zero, it returns zero.	>> a = [5 0 14 0 0 13]; >> any ans =1 >> b = [0 0 0 0 0]; >> any(b) ans = 0
find(a) find(a>d)	Returns the indices of the nonzero vector elements Yes, a is a vector; find returns the indices of elements that are greater than d (You can use any other relational operator than a>d)	>> a = [0 7 4 2 8 0 0 3 9]; >> find(a) ans =2 3 4 5 8 9 >> find(a>4) ans=2 5 9

Examples:

1. The maximum temperatures from February 1 to 28 have been:

15, 14, 10, 12, 6, 8, 12, 16, 18, 20, 17, 15, 13, 11, 9, 7, 5, 4, 6, 8, 12, 13, 15, 19, 21, 23, 16, 14

Determine the number of days and the dates on which the maximum temperature of the day is greater than or equal to 15 degrees Celsius

As we have seen, T>=15 is a vector whose elements take the value one if the condition is met and 0 otherwise.

```
>> T=[15 14 10 12 6 8 12 16 18 20 17 15 13 11 9 7 5 4 6 8 12 13 15
19 21 23 16 14];
>> length(T)
ans = 28
>> days=sum(T>=15)
days = 11
>> dates=find(T>=15) %indices of the elements of the vector T that are >= than 15
dates =
    1 8 9 10 11 12 23 24 25 26 27
>> length(dates)
ans = 11
```

In the case of the function, all can be used in sentences of this type: If all the elements of the vector a are greater than one, do some homework. Similarly, you can use the function any.

if all(a>1)

do something

end

2. In the following vector, save the ages of several people: age=[45,47,15,23,7,60,35,28,32,10,41]. Determine

The total number of people,

```
>> age=[45,47,15,23,7,60,35,28,32,10,41];
>> length(age)
ans = 11
```

- Who are adults (mark with a one), and the number of adults over 20 years of age,

```
>> adults=age>20
adults = 1 1 0 1 0 1 1 1 1 0 1
>> n_adults=sum(adults)
n_adults = 8
```

- Who are the children, and what is the number of children ten years old or younger?

```
>> children=age<=10
children = 0 0 0 0 1 0 0 0 0 1 0
>> n_children=sum(children)
n_children = 2
```

- Who are young people and the number of young people over ten years of age and up to and including 20 years of age

```
>> youth=age>10 & age<=20
youth = 0 0 1 0 0 0 0 0 0 0 0
>> n_young=sum(young)
n_youth = 1
>> n_children+n_adults+n_youth
ans = 11
```

- Is there a child?

```
>> any(age<=10)
ans = 1
```

- Are they all adults?

```
>> all(age>20)
ans = 0
```

We create a data vector of people's weights: weight=[70,83,45,60,25,55,90,73,65,35,78]

- How many adults weigh more than 65 kg?

```
>> age=[45,47,15,23,7,60,35,28,32,10,41];
>> weight=[70,83,45,60,25,55,90,73,65,35,78];
>> age>20
ans = 1 1 0 1 0 1 1 1 1 0 1
>> weight>65
ans = 1 1 0 0 0 0 1 1 0 0 1
>> age>20 & weight>65
ans = 1 1 0 0 0 0 1 1 0 0 1
>> sum(age>20 & weight>65)
ans = 5
```

- Use find to create a vector of Adults of adult ages

```
>> age=[45,47,15,23,7,60,35,28,32,10, 41];
>> find(age>20)
ans = 1 2 4 6 7 8 9 11
>> adults=age(find(age>20))
adults = 45 47 23 60 35 28 32 41
>> length(adults)
ans = 8
```

- Determine the weight of the third adult in the vector Adults

```
>> age=[45,47,15,23,7,60,35,28,32,10,41];
>> weight=[70,83,45,60,25,55,90,73,65,35,78];
>> indices=find(age>20)
indices = 1 2 4 6 7 8 9 11
>> weight(indexes(3))
ans = 60
```

3. Given the vector v=1:16;

```
>> v
v = 1 2 3 4 5 6 7 8 9 10 11 12 13 14 15 16
```

- They show even numbers greater than 4

```
>> v(rem(v,2)==0 & v>4)
ans = 6 8 10 12 14 16
```

- Remove from vector v all elements that are multiples of three.

```
>> v=1:16;
>> v(rem(v,3)==0)=[]
v = 1 2 4 5 7 8 10 11 13 14 16
```

4. A company pays the following types of annual salary: 12,000, 15,000, 18,000, 24,000, 35,000, 50,000, and 70,000. The number of employees in each category is 3,000, 2,500, 1,500, 1,000, 400, 100, and 25. Calculate:
   - The total number of employees
   - The number of company employees whose salaries are more than 32000 and less than that amount
   - The average salary per employee in the company (weighted average)

```
>> salary=[12000,15000,18000,24000,35000,50000,70000];
>> employees=[3000,2500,1500,1000,400,100,25];
>> n_employees=sum(employees)
n_employees = 8525
>> u=salary>32000
u = 0 0 0 0 1 1 1
>> u.*employees
ans = 0 0 0 0 400 100 25
>> n_height=sum(u.*employees)
n_height = 525
>> n_low=n_employees-n_high
n_low = 8000
>> average_salary=sum(employees.*salary)/n_employees
median_salary = 1.7038e+004
```

5. The electricity bill of residents in a certain city is calculated as follows:
   - If 500 Kwh or less is consumed, the cost is 2 cents per kWh

- If more than 500 Kwh are consumed but not more than 1000, the cost is 10 euros for the first 500 Kwh and 5 cents per kWh for consumption that exceeds 500 Kwh
- If more than 1,000 Kwh are consumed, the cost is 35 euros for the first 1,000 Kwh and 10 cents per kWh for consumption that exceeds 1,000 Kwh.
- The electricity company includes a fixed cost of 5 euros, regardless of consumption.

The readings of the electricity meter of five families have been the following: 200, 500, 700, 1000, and 1500 Kwh, respectively. Show the calculation results in two columns, one for consumption and the other for the cost of electricity consumed.

```
consumption=[200,500,700,1000,1500];
cost=5+10*(consumption>500)+25*(consumption>1000);
cost=cost+0.02*(consumption<=500).*consumption;
cost=cost+0.05*(consumption>500 & consumption<=1000).*(consumption-500);
cost=cost+0.1*(consumption>1000).*(consumption-1000);
disp([consumption',cost'])
    200 9
    500 15
    700 25
    1000 40
    1500 90
```

Chapter 3: SQL With Applications

One of the many advantages of SQL database management systems is their ease of configuration and ease of use. In addition, some systems are freely accessible, such as MySQL, which makes them especially accessible for small and medium-sized companies with limited resources.

MySQL is also very secure thanks to its strong data security levels, cross-platform compatibility, and speed and scalability. This makes it the most popular database management system, along with Microsoft SQL Server; it is used by multi-billion dollar companies like Facebook, Twitter, and YouTube, as well as thousands of SMEs.

In addition, SQL database systems are also widely used in various industries such as finance, manufacturing, insurance, healthcare, and more.

That being said, SQL also has its limits. If, for example, you want to visualize data with SQL, you will have to adopt other tools, that is, integrate with external libraries in Python such as Matplotlib, D3.js in JavaScript, or others. Unlike SQL, which is quite easy to use, these tools significantly need more knowledge and experience.

This is where Open as App can come in handy. If you need the ability to visualize and analyze your data similarly to Excel through charts and diagrams, you might consider creating an app with your SQL data.

Plus, with an app, you can also share your enhanced data with others, which can help you use that data more productively—and in new ways.

Why build a mobile app from your SQL data?

Open as App allows you to add a layer of functionality on top of the various ways you are already using your data with your database management system. By creating an application through SQL data, you can.

- Share data in a comprehensive and user-friendly way
- Protect data from tampering and corruption while disclosing it to stakeholders with an application instead of an open export file
- Select the specific data you want to display and leave the rest out
- Deliver information in a user-friendly way while adding data evaluation capabilities to your App (such as automated list analysis)

You can also insert Excel logic to your SQL data with Open as App. This allows you to enhance data with functionality not otherwise accessible in DBMS.

For example, by inserting Excel logic, you can add dashboards, charts, and diagrams to your application that were not previously part of the data in its SQL format. Action buttons, such as a print functionality, allow the export of the data to a PDF file and can be added.

Advantages of using Open as an App for the creation of SQL applications

The implementation of the Open as App platform in your operations does not change your current IT infrastructure or how data is managed and used. Open as App does not replace any of your systems but is an additional tool to work, analyze and visualize the data.

Some of the advantages of using Open as an App in your company are

- It takes very little time and resources to create applications with Open as App, compared to the standard ways of developing applications
- The low effort from enterprise IT departments while ensuring full control of application development, management, access, and publishing
- Add evaluation and analytical logic to Microsoft Excel in no time and improve data productivity
- Easy application maintenance and deployment of application updates
- App creation can be collaborative and lead to new ways of understanding and using data, increasing productivity and innovation.

These benefits, especially for small and medium-sized businesses, come immediately from implementing Open as App. So, do you want to try building an app with SQL data?

Here's how to go from SQL to an application in minutes.

How to create a mobile application based on SQL data?

Here's how to build your first App from SQL data. Following the steps described below, you can use your data or, if you wish, the demo data we have made available to you.

Connect your data to Open as App

You must go through the Open as App wizard to build an app with your SQL data. After the initial registration, you'll be prompted to choose your data source. Select the "MS SQL, MySQL, REST" option from the menu at this stage. Open as App is also compatible with PostgreSQL.

Load the spreadsheet to create a base application

Once you've selected SQL as your data source, you'll need to select your data provider. If you want to work with your data, select your provider.

If you'd like to try converting your SQL data to an application using the Open as App demo data instead, select Microsoft SQL Server, click "Connect," and then the "Use our demo account" button."

Select the tables and data fields for the database app

Once you've connected to your provider or selected the demo data option, you can select the tables and fields you need to add to your App.

In the case of demo data, it is provided the option of working with the data of a store manager managing your products and sales. As you will see, there are some different tables that you can select from.

When selecting a particular table, you will be given the option to choose the fields you want to include in your application. If you require to include more than one Table, click on the "Click here to add data" button, which will redirect back to the list of tables.

Add a custom query

As you'll see above the tables, you're also given the option to add a custom query if you need one. Of course, your IT administrator or company SQL expert is where you should go for help for those who aren't SQL users.

A custom query will allow you, for example, to limit the data fields that a user sees. You may need to do this for security and practical reasons: Since a database can have tens of thousands of data entries, limiting visibility and access will make the application more usable.

Enhance with Excel logic (optional)

If you want to add more than just your SQL data in list form to your application, you can also select the "Enhance with Excel logic" option from the same screen at this stage.

You will then be directed to download the data in spreadsheet form and add any calculations, formulas, tables, or graphs you want to include in your application. Now you must not edit any sheets that comprise your data. In its place, create new sheets for any calculations or additions you want.

Once you've added the Excel functions you want in your App, upload the spreadsheet again to Open as App, and proceed to build your App.

Build your mobile App from SQL

If you decide not to add the Excel logic to your data, click the "Next" button, and you will be taken to the next step in the app creation process.

If the spreadsheet is downloaded with your SQL data to enhance it with Excel, you will need to upload it in the app wizard. After clicking "Next," you will also be taken to the next stage of the application creation process.

Creating an app through our app creation wizard is very intuitive and easy. If you have any remaining questions about the process, check out our App Creation 101 guide for an overview.

Characteristics of an SQL application

List applications are the most common type of application built with SQL data. When you create such an app, these are some of the features it can have:

- Chart analysis – once the platform analyzes your data, you will be given the option to convert the data into various charts.
- Different views – one can select how you want to display your data – as a list, a grid list, a card list, or as charts
- Sorting and grouping: you can sort and group your data according to your preferences
- In-app calling: If your data contains phone numbers, you can enable in-app calling.
- Different data formats – Various formats will be recognized by the Open as an App platform.

Finally, you can create other applications with Open as App by enhancing your data with Excel logic. You can create a calculator application using your initial SQL data to add formulas and calculations with Microsoft Excel. On the other hand, if you add tables and charts with Excel, you can create a dashboard app based on your data.

Chapter 4: Data Persistence

Persistence is the ability to save a program's information so it can be used again later. It is what users know as saving the file and then Opening it. But to a programmer, it can mean more things. It usually involves serializing the data to a file, a database, or some other similar medium and the reverse process of retrieving the data from the serialized information.

For example, suppose that in the development of a game, you want to save in a file the information referring to the winners, the maximum score obtained, and the game time in which they obtained that score.

In-game, that information could be stored in a list of tuples:

[(name1, score1, time1), (name2, score2, time2), ...]

This information can be saved to a file in many different ways. In this case, to make the scores file easier to read for humans, it is decided to save them in a text file, where each tuple will occupy one line, and commas will separate the values of the tuples.

Code shows a module capable of saving and retrieving scores in the specified format.

Given the problem's specifications, saving the values to the file requires converting the score (which is a numeric value) to a string, and opening the file requires converting it back to a numeric value.

Note: It is important to note that both the function that stores the data and the one that retrieves it requires that the information be found in a certain way; if it is not, it will fail. That is why these conditions are indicated in the functions' documentation as their preconditions. In future units, we will see how to prevent a function from failing if its conditions are not met.

It's pretty easy to test the scripted module and see that what is saved is the same as what is retrieved:

scores.py: Module to save and retrieve scores to a file

```python
#! /usr/bin/env python
# encoding: latin1
def save_scores (file_name, scores) :
    """ Saves the list of scores to the file.
    Pre: file_name corresponds to a valid file,
        scores corresponds to a list of 3-tuples.
    Post: values were saved to the file,
        separated by commas.
    """
    file = open(file_name, "w" )
    for name, score, time in scores:
        file.write(name+ "," +str(score)+ "," +time+ "\\n" )
    file.close()
```

```python
def retrieve_scores (file_name) :
    """ Retrieves scores from the provided file.
    Returns a list with the values of the scores.
    Pre: the file contains the scores in the expected format,
        separated by commas
    Post: The returned list contains the scores in the format:
        [(name1,score1,time1),(name2,score2,time2)].
    """

    scores = []
    file = open(file_name, "r" )
    for line in file:
        name, score, time = line.rstrip( "\\n" ).split( "," )
        scores.append((name,int(score),time))
    file.close()
    return scores
>>> import scores
>>> values = [( "Pepe" , 108 , "4:16" ), ( "Juana" , 2315 , "8:4
>>> scores.save_scores( "scores .txt " , values)
>>> retrieved = scores.retrieve_scores( "scores.txt" )
>>> print retrieved
[( 'Pepe' , 108 , '4:16' ), ( 'Joan' , 2315 , '8:42' )]
```

Saving the state of a program can be done in both a text file and a binary file. In many situations, it is preferable to save the information in a text file since, in this way, it is possible to modify it from any text editor easily.

In general, text files will waste a little more space, but they are easier to understand and use from within any program.

On the other hand, in a well-defined binary file, you can avoid wasting space or make it faster to access data. Also, it would make little sense to store certain applications like sound or video files in text files.

Ultimately, the decision of which format to use is left to the programmer's discretion. It is important to remember that common sense is the most precious asset in a programmer.

Persistence in CSV files

A format that is often used to transfer data between programs is CSV (comma-separated values: values separated by commas) is a fairly simple format, both to read and to process from the Code; it is similar to the format seen in the example above.

```
Name, Surname, Telephone, Birthday
"John","Smith","555-0101","1973-11-24"
"Jane","Smith","555-0101","1975-06-12"
```

In the example, you can see a small database. In the first line of the file, we have the names of the fields, an optional piece of information from the point of view of information processing, which makes it easier to understand the file.

The data from the database is entered in the following lines, each field separated by commas. Fields that are strings are usually written in double quotes; if any string contains a double quote, it is replaced by \", and a backslash is written as \\.

In Python, it is quite easy to process these files for reading and writing using the module csv that is already prepared for that.

The functions of the previous example could be programmed using the CSV module. A possible implementation using this module is shown in the Code below.

Trying this Code returns identical output to the one obtained above:

```
>>> import csv_scores
>>> values = [( "Pepe" , 108 , "4:16" ), ( "Juana" , 2315 , "8:42" )]
>>> csv_scores.save_scores( "scores .txt " , values)
>>> retrieved = scores_csv.recover_scores( "scores.txt" )
>>> print retrieved
[( 'Pepe' , 108 , '4:16' ), ( 'Joan' , 2315 , '8:42' )]
```

The Code, in this case, is very similar since, in the original example, very little consideration was made about the values: the first and third were assumed to be a string. In contrast, the second needed to be converted to a string.

scores_csv.py: Module to save and retrieve scores to a file using CSV

```python
#! /usr/bin/env python
# encoding: latin1
import csv
def save_scores (file_name, scores) :
    """ Saves the list of scores to the file.
    Pre: file_name corresponds to a valid file,
        scores correspond to a list of sequences of elements.
    Post: values were saved to the file,
        separated by commas.
    """

    file = open(file_name, "w" )
    csv_file = csv.writer(file)
    csv_file.writerrows(scores)
    file.close()


def retrieve_scores (file_name) :
    """ Retrieves scores from the provided file.
    Returns a list with the values of the scores.
    Pre: the file contains the scores in the expected format,
        separated by commas
    Post: The returned list contains the scores in the format:
        [(name1,score1,time1),(name2,score2,time2)].
    """

    scores = []
    file = open(file_name, "r" )
    csv_file = csv.reader(file)
    for name, score, time in csv_file:
        scores.append((name, int(score), time))
    file.close()
    return scores
```

Note: It is important to note that using the CSV module instead of manually processing results in more robust behavior since the module takes many more cases into account than our original Code did not. For example, the Code above did not consider that the name might contain a comma.

A full scheduler application, which stores program data in CSV files, can be seen in the appendix to this unit.

Persistence in binary files

If we decide to record the data in a binary file, Python includes a pickle tool that makes it very easy. Keep in mind, however, that it is not easy to access a file in this format from a program that is not written in Python.

The same example of storing scores is shown in the Code below, using the pickle.

scores_pickle.py: Module for saving and retrieving scores to a file using pickle

```
#! /usr/bin/env python
# encoding: latin1
imported pickles
def save_scores (file_name, scores) :
    """ Saves the list of scores to the file.
    Pre: file_name corresponds to a valid file,
        scores correspond to the values to save
    Post: Saved the values to the file in pickle format.
    """
    file = open(file_name, "w" )
    pickle.dump(scores, file)
    file.close()
def retrieve_scores (file_name) :
    """ Retrieves scores from the provided file.
    Returns a list with the values of the scores.
    Pre: file contains scores in pickle format
    Post: The returned list contains the scores in the
        same format in which they were stored.
    """
    file = open(file_name, "r" )
    scores = pickle.load(file)
    file.close()
    return scores
```

The operation of this program will be identical to the previous ones. But the generated file will be very different from the previously generated files. Instead of being a readable file, it will take the form:

```
(lp0
(S'Pepe'
p1
I108
S'4:16'
p2
tp3
to(S'Juana'
p4
I2315
S'8:42'
p5
tp6
```

Chapter 5: Triggers in SQL

Triggers are database entities in SQL Server. Technically, they are a particular class of function calls that respond to specific database operations.

This essential guide will give you detailed information on SQL Triggers that can be useful in your profession. Let us begin!

What are SQL Triggers?

The word "trigger" describes a statement that a server automatically executes the query whenever the content of the database is changed.

A trigger is a group of SQL Queries stored in memory space. It is a specific function call immediately whenever a database event occurs. Each trigger has a table assigned to it.

For example, a trigger could be fired whenever a new column is added to a particular table or if specific records are modified.

According to the Microsoft Developer Network, triggers are a particular class of stored procedures. In a trigger declaration, we initially define when the trigger should run and then provide the action to take after the trigger has fired.

Syntax:

```
CREATE TRIGGER trigger_name
BEFORE/AFTER
INSERT/UPDATE/DELETE
ON tableName
FOR EACH ROW SET operation [trigger_body];
```

Explanation of each parameter

- CREATE TRIGGER trigger_name – Used to build or rename an existing trigger.
- BEFORE AFTER – This query is used to define the execution time of the trigger (before or after a certain event).
- INSERT / UPDATE / DELETE – This describes the action we want to perform on the tables.
- ON tableName – Here, we define the Table's name to configure a trigger.
- PER ROW – This statement is related to the row trigger, which means that the triggers will be executed every time a row is modified.
- body_trigger – Specifies the action to perform when the trigger is activated.

Triggers are functions stored with distinctive identities that allow us to reuse queries that have already been executed and stored safely in memory. Now let's try to understand why SQL needs them.

Triggers are mainly used to regulate the implementation of Code each time an event occurs. Put another way; triggers are ideal if you constantly need a specific piece of Code to execute in response to a specific event.

The following are some benefits of using triggers on SQL database operations.

1. Performs additional checks when inserting, updating, or deleting data from the affected Table.
2. Reduce response times, which helps increase IT expenses.
3. Enables encoding of sophisticated default parameters that are inaccessible by initial constraints.

Referential integrity is a key core property of relational database systems. This means that the data stored in the database system must always be accurate for each transaction and each operation.

If two tables are located in separate databases or systems, there is no way to ensure data validation within them using constraint values. In such a situation, triggers are the only option for execution.

Combination of Trigger Arguments

For each Table, we can specify six different types of triggers. These combine the Trigger arguments included in the SQL Row Level Triggers.

BEFORE INSERT – These triggers execute the action on the rows before any INSERT operations are performed on the specified Table or database.

AFTER INSERT: Executes the action on the rows immediately after any INSERT activity from the database.

BEFORE UPDATE: With these triggers, a function is performed on the rows before an UPDATE action is performed on the database.

AFTER UPDATE: Acts on the rows immediately following any database or table-specific UPDATE activity.

BEFORE DELETE: Performs a certain operation on the rows even before the database or Table undergoes a DELETE action.

AFTER DELETE: These triggers execute the action on the rows following each transaction.

Types of SQL Triggers

SQL triggers are stored functions that are executed immediately when specific events occur. It is similar to event-based programming. Following situations can initiate the execution of triggers.

DML Triggers – DML stands for Data Manipulation Language. Code execution in reaction to data modification is made possible by DML Triggers. This trigger fires when DML commands such as INSERT, UPDATE, and DELETE are executed. These are also called "table-level triggers."

DDL Triggers – DDL stands for Data Definition Language. DDL triggers allow us to execute Code in reaction to changes in the database schema, such as adding or deleting tables, or server events, such as when a user logs in. These are called "Database Level Triggers."

These triggers can be fired when certain DDL statements like CREATE, ALTER, or DROP are executed on the active database. These can also be used to control and manage running activities.

Login Triggers – The login triggers are immediately invoked whenever an event log (boot, login, logout, shutdown) occurs. They are only performed after a user authentication process, even before the user transaction is started. LOGIN triggers will not fire if authorization fails.

These triggers can record login history or set an event restriction for a particular login, among other auditing and identity management functions for server connections.

CLR Triggers – CLR stands for Common Language Runtime. CLR triggers are a unique subset built primarily on CLR within .NET technology. These triggers are useful if the trigger needs to do a lot of computation or needs to relate to a non-SQL entity.

DML and DDL triggers can be built by enabling the coding of supported CLR triggers in .NET technologies, including Visual Basic, C#, and F-sharp.

Sample SQL Server Trigger

Let's understand these triggering concepts with an example.

First, let's create a database using SQL statements.

```
CREATE DATABASE testdb;
use testdb;
```

Here, I have given a "testdb" as the database name. And the next step is to create a table.

```
CREATE TABLE student(
name varchar(25),
id int(2),
maths int(2),
physics int(2),
biology int(2),
social int(2),
total int(2)
);
```

I have created a table to store the details of the students. And here is the command to describe the structure of the Table. Here "student" is the name of the Table that I have given.

DESC student;

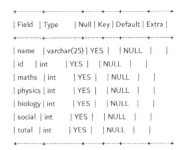

Here is the table structure that I have created.

After creating a table, the next step is to set up a trigger. Let's try using the BEFORE INSERT argument.

The name of the trigger I have created is "marks." As soon as the Table with the student's grades is modified, the trigger below automatically tries to determine the student's overall grade.

```
CREATE TRIGGER marks
BEFORE INSERT
ON
student
FOR EACH ROW
set new.total=new.maths+new.physics+new.biology+new.social;
```

Because we need to replace the data in the rows instead of working with the old, we've defined "total" with a new class name, and all subsequent expressions are prefixed with new keywords after the total using the dot operator. Now, we'll add values to each row and see the results. Initially, the total mark is 0 for each student.

```
INSERT INTO student VALUES("George",02,99,87,92,91,0);
INSERT INTO student VALUES("James",03,91,81,94,90,0);
INSERT INTO student VALUES("Harry",04,86,70,73,88,0);
INSERT INTO student VALUES("John",05,73,89,78,92,0);
INSERT INTO student VALUES("Lisa",01,94,75,69,79,0);
```

The trigger statement will be triggered automatically when data is inserted into the student table. The trigger will calculate the total grades for each student. Now, let's see whether or not the trigger is called using a SELECT.

SELECT * FROM table_name;

And here is the result.

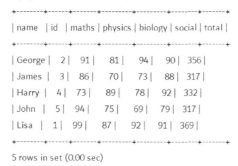

```
mysql> select * from student;
+--------+----+-------+---------+---------+--------+-------+
| name   | id | maths | physics | biology | social | total |
+--------+----+-------+---------+---------+--------+-------+
| George |  2 |   91  |    81   |    94   |   90   |  356  |
| James  |  3 |   86  |    70   |    73   |   88   |  317  |
| Harry  |  4 |   73  |    89   |    78   |   92   |  332  |
| John   |  5 |   94  |    75   |    69   |   79   |  317  |
| Lisa   |  1 |   99  |    87   |    92   |   91   |  369  |
+--------+----+-------+---------+---------+--------+-------+
5 rows in set (0.00 sec)
```

In the output above, you can see that all subject grades are automatically added for each student. So, we can conclude that the trigger was successfully invoked.

Additional Trigger Operations

We can perform many operations using triggers. Some may be simple, and others a bit complex, but once we go through the queries, it's easy to understand. Using Transact-SQL statements, you can enable, disable, or remove triggers using the following commands.

Query to check if a specific trigger is there or not

This command searches the entire database for the specified trigger.

SELECT * FROM [sys].[triggers] WHERE [name] = 'Trigger_name.'

Query to show triggers

All triggers in the active database will be displayed in the following statement.

SHOW TRIGGERS;

Query to disable the trigger

The following command disables the trigger on the working database.

DISABLE TRIGGER trigger_name ON DATABASE;

You can also specify a particular table name to disable a trigger.

DISABLE TRIGGER trigger_name ON table_name;

Query to enable trigger

The following command disables a specific trigger defined on the specified Table in the active database before re-enabling it.

ALTER TABLE table_name DISABLE TRIGGER trigger_name

ALTER TABLE table_name ENABLE TRIGGER trigger_name

The trigger must be disabled before trying to enable it,

Query to enable or disable all triggers on a table

Using the above SQL statement, we can disable or enable all table triggers at once by substituting "ALL" in place of a specific trigger name.

ALTER TABLE table_name DISABLE TRIGGER ALL

ALTER TABLE table_name ENABLE TRIGGER ALL

Query to remove or discard trigger

A trigger can be deleted by deleting it or deleting the entire Table. Each related trigger is also dropped when a table is dropped.

DROP TRIGGER [trigger_name];

The related data is removed from the sys whenever a trigger is removed. Objects data table.

Advantages of Triggers

- Creating triggers is easy; the trigger can call stored functions and methods.
- Users can implement simple auditing using triggers.
- Tragically, you cannot create cross-entity constraints on SQL Server database systems, although you can emulate how constraints work using triggers.
- Integrity constraints can be implemented in databases using triggers.
- Triggers can be useful when group validation is required rather than a row-by-row check of newly entered or changed data.

Disadvantages of Triggers

SQL triggers may not be the best option in some situations due to their limitations.

- Triggers must be accurately documented.
- Due to the concurrent execution of the database that application components may not be able to access, triggers can be difficult to debug.
- DML declarations become more complex when triggers are used.
- Even a minor trigger problem has the potential to lead to logical failures in the statement.

Conclusion

Triggers are useful components of Transact-SQL and SQL; you can also use them in Oracle. The use of triggers is crucial when calling stored methods. These SQL Triggers allow us to analyze activity schedules and determine how to respond to them if necessary. We can also search for a certain table connected to a trigger to acquire data.

Triggers can enable recursion. Every time a trigger on a table executes a command on the parent table, the second iteration of the trigger fires, known as a recursive trigger. This helps when trying to resolve an identity mapping.

Additionally, triggers regulate the updated pattern that the database can accept. Maintaining data integrity constraints in the database system is very beneficial if the SQL constraint keys do not exist, mainly the primary and foreign keys.

Chapter 6: Combining equal queries in SQL

In standard SQL data query language, the UNION operator combines the results of two independent queries, returning all the records returned by both as the joint result.

To perform the union, both queries must return the same fields, their names, and the data type. What is not necessary is that they are obtained in the same way. Some could be direct fields obtained from a query to a table, and those in the second part could be calculated fields. As long as they have the same name and type, there is no problem.

So in the simplest case, for example, if we have two information tables with sales data separated by divisions, something like this (in two different tables):

SalesSoftware	
Commercial	**Sales**
Peter	1000
Sarah	1500
Maria	2000

SalesConsultation	
Commercial	**Sales**
Eva	2000
Monica	1250
Peter	1000

We can write a query like this:

```
SELECT Comercial, Sales FROM SalesSoftware
UNION
SELECT Comercial, Sales FROM SalesConsultation
```

To get the combined result of both tables:

Commercial	Sales
Peter	1000
Sarah	1500
Maria	2000
Eva	2000
Monica	1250

Here is an important detail. If we look at these results, we will see that Pepe, who is in both tables with the same sales value, only appears once. And it is that UNION avoids that there are duplicate records in the final result. It removes duplicate rows where all the field values are the same.

```
SELECT Comercial, Sales From SalesSoftware
UNIONALL
SELECT Comercial, Sales FROM SalesConsultation
```

If we want to get the total mix, even with duplicates, we must use UNION ALL :

Commercial	Sales
Peter	1000
Sarah	1500
Maria	2000
Eva	2000
Monica	1250
Peter	1000

Which, in this case, returns us:

In this case, we see how the commercial " Peter" is twice.

Apart from this obvious one, there is another very important difference between the two methods: UNION ALL offers much more performance than UNION. The reason is that the process is much simpler by not discriminating between repeated records. In regular queries with few records, we won't notice it, but in large queries with many possible results, it will.

Also, if we're sure that the two result sets we're joining don't have common data (or don't care), it's better to always use UNION ALL for this reason.

Cross-reference query in SQL Server

1. The problem.

When working with daily capture data such as sales, it is common to be asked for cross-reference reports, for example, to convert this data

customer	date	amount	(other columns)
JOSEPH	2006-06-01	1000.0	
JOSEPH	2006-06-02	2000.0	
JOSEPH	2006-06-03	3000.0	
LEWIS	2006-06-01	12000.0	
LEWIS	2006-06-02	32000.0	
LEWIS	2006-06-03	35000.0	
LEWIS	2006-06-04	12500.0	
PACO	2006-06-01	12000.0	
PACO	2006-06-02	32000.0	
LUZMA	2006-06-01	4000.0	
LUZMA	2006-06-02	6300.0	

In this:

Customer	06/01/2006	06/02/2006	06/03/2006	06/04/2006	Total
JOSEPH	1000.0	2000.0	3000.0	2500.0	8500.0
LEWIS	12000.0	32000.0	35000.0	12500.0	91500.0
LUZMA	4000.0	6300.0	2000.0	1500.0	13800.0
PACO	12000.0	32000.0	35000.0	12500.0	91500.0

2. The solution.

This approach uses physical tables to filter and convert the data and accumulate the results. The first attempt I made was with temporary tables and in-memory tables. Still, it gave me strange errors when trying to delete and recreate the temporary tables or add the columns dynamically in the in-memory tables.

The first step is to create a table that contains only the necessary columns and rows. In this way, the use of server resources is optimized. We will create a table containing the customer, date, and amount columns:

The purpose of creating the date column as varchar is to make it easier to create later columns in the result table.

```
if exists (select * from dbo.sysobjects
    where id = object_id(N'[dbo].[tab1]') and OBJECTPROPERTY(id, N'IsTable') = 1)
    drop table [dbo].[tab1]
GO
-- note: in this the date is nvarchar
CREATE TABLE tab1(customer nvarchar(50) NOT NULL, date nvarchar(10) NOT NULL,
    actual amount NULL)
GO
```

The records are inserted below; suppose the source table is called EXAMPLE:

```
INSERT INTO tab1 (customer, date,
   amount)
SELECT customer, CONVERT(nvarchar(10),date,103), amount
FROM example
WHERE date BETWEEN '06/01/2006' AND '06/04/2006'
```

Now the results table is created, which initially includes only the customers:

```
if exists (select * from dbo.sysobjects
   where id = object_id(N'[dbo].[tab2]') and OBJECTPROPERTY(id, N'IsTable') = 1)
   drop table [dbo].[tab2]
   GO
CREATE TABLE tab2 (Client nvarchar(50) NOT NULL )
   GO
```

The already filtered clients are inserted:

```
INSERT INTO tab2 (Client)
SELECT DISTINCT customer FROM tab1
```

The next step is more complex and includes using a cursor to read the different dates to be added and the execution of queries "on the fly" using the EXECUTE statement.

The logic is:

- Consult the different dates of the filtered Table.
- For each date, insert a column.
- Update that column with the selected date's value from the filtered Table.

```
-- variable to create the columns
DECLARE @head nvarchar(50)
-- variables to define queries at runtime
DECLARE @exec1 nvarchar(1024)
DECLARE @exec2 nvarchar(1024)
-- declare the cursor
DECLARE CURSOR FOR headers
   SELECT DISTINCT date FROM tab1
-- open cursor
OPEN headers
FETCH NEXT FROM headers INTO @headers
-- as long as there is data...
WHILE @@FETCH_STATUS = 0
BEGIN
   -- for each date, add a column
   SET @exec1 = 'ALTER TABLE tab2 ADD [' + @header + '] real NULL '
   EXECUTE (@exec1)
   -- update new column with values
   SET @exec2 = 'UPDATE tab2 SET [' + @header + '] = t1.amount ' +
      ' FROM tab1 t1 INNER JOIN tab2 t2 ON t1.customer=t2.customer ' +
      ' WHERE t1.date=''' + @head + ''''
   EXECUTE (@exec2)
   -- next record
   FETCH NEXT FROM headers INTO @headers
END
-- close and free cursor memory
CLOSE headers
DEALOCATE headers
```

Note using two single quotes to delimit the @head criteria since it is a string.

At this time, the Table already contains the data ready to display using a SELECT. However, to complete the example, we will aggregate the totals per row using a third table:

```
if exists (select * from dbo.sysobjects where id = object_id(N'[dbo].[tab3]')
and
OBJECTPROPERTY(id, N'IsTable') = 1)
drop table [dbo].[tab3]
GO
CREATE TABLE tab3 (client nvarchar(50) NOT NULL, actual total NULL)
GO
-- insert customers and totals
INSERT INTO tab3 (customer, total)
SELECT customer, sum(amount) FROM tab1 GROUP BY customer
```

A column of totals is added to the results table and is

updated with the newly created Table:

```
-- create column of totals
ALTER TABLE tab2 ADD Actual Total NULL
-- update totals
DECLARE @exec3 nvarchar(1024)
SET @exec3 ='UPDATE tab2 SET total= t3.total ' +
   ' FROM tab2 t2 INNER JOIN tab3 t3 ON t2.customer=t3.customer'
EXECUTE (@exec3)
```

SELECT * FROM tab2

It should be noted that this last query must be carried out at runtime so that the procedure is compiled correctly since the TOTAL column is added dynamically. Otherwise, the query analyzer detects that the TOTAL column does not exist and returns an error. This is why the EXECUTE statement is used.

Finally, to display the results, execute a simple SELECT:

Conclusion.

A technique has been demonstrated that combines temporary tables and a cursor to create a crosstab where the column names are not known in advance, in a common usage scenario in most applications.

The advantage of creating the columns in order is that the presentation is considerably simplified since it is not required to carry out complicated operations when displaying the results. A data grid can be used to create the columns automatically.

The disadvantage of this approach is that you have to use physical tables to accumulate the results. It remains to solve this problem using temporary tables (of the form #tab1), or objects in memory, using the syntax DECLARE @tab1 TABLE (customer int NOT NUL, date varchar (10), actual amount).

A text file with the query is appended and executed in the parser. A note is included at the end to convert the query to a stored procedure. This can be used to run the query from within an ASP.NET application. The dataset it returns can be assigned to a dataset and assigned to that dataset as a data source for a data grid; well, I guess you know the rest of the story.

Chapter 7: Big Data Tools to Achieve Better Results

In Big Data, having better, quality data is essential, as much or more than having an expert Data Scientist who knows how to extract value from the information provided by that data or having a manager willing to take risks by adopting Big projects. Dating for your business, it is equally essential to have the most appropriate Big Data tools to develop the Big Data solutions necessary to achieve the best possible results.

Analytical techniques and all their revolution are nothing if we do not have a good list of Big Data tools to store the data, such as an adequate database, data processing, and management tools, to be able to carry out specific queries, analysis tools of data, to detect patterns that no one else can see, or data visualization tools, to clarify the results, all of them at the service of our business with the sole objective of improving results.

Big Data tools to store data

A couple of decades ago, a terabyte was almost unimaginable information. Today, however, many data centers are measured in petabytes, even zettabytes. Storing such an overwhelming amount of data requires tools with enormous capacity. In this context, databases play a key role.

Databases are a compendium of data related to the same context and massively stored for later use. Most of the databases are already in digital format, which allows them to be processed by computer and accessed in less time. They can hold both structured and unstructured information. In computing, due to their way of structuring the information and the language they use, they are broadly classified into SQL and NoSQL databases.

SQL databases

SQL databases (Structured Query Language or structured query language) use a declarative language for accessing relational databases that allow queries to store, modify and extract information.

The main characteristic is that SQL databases follow a standard, both in the way they are designed and in the way they store information and in which they must be consulted.

All SQL databases comply with ACID properties (Atomicity of operations, Consistency of data, Isolation of concurrent operations, and Durability of data). Some examples: DB2, Oracle, SQLite….

NoSQL databases

NoSQL databases (MongoDB, Cassandra, Elasticsearch, Cloudant, Neo4j, Redis) do not require fixed structures and are classified according to their way of storing the data in document, columnar, or graph databases.

NoSQL databases are characterized by being much more heterogeneous. They are all those that do not follow the SQL standard and, therefore, do not meet any of the ACID properties.

They are more flexible when storing data of various kinds or massive data that must be shared among multiple machines. In return, they do not guarantee that the data is always available in its most up-to-date version, and they are usually limited to simpler queries than those done on SQL databases.

SQL or no SQL? That is the question. In general, choosing SQL or NoSQL will depend on the type of product we are building, although due to the nature of Big Data projects, NoSQL is usually more convenient.

Big Data tools to process data

All the infrastructures destined to manage and process data, such as open source frameworks (Open Source) such as Hadoop, Apache Spark, Storm, or Kafka, constitute high-performance technological platforms designed for manipulating data sources, either in batch processing. Or in real-time.

These ecosystems are also characterized by the programming language on which their operation is based. These languages are designed to accurately express algorithms and test, debug, and maintain the source code of a computer program. Today the most used in Big Data are Python, Java, R, and Scala.

Big Data tools to analyze data

The basis of Big Data techniques lies in the tools for data analysis. Unlike data storage and processing, analytics tools are not as standardized.

A good data scientist will normally combine different Open Source tools and packages to apply the most appropriate algorithms to the problem they are working on.

For this, advanced mathematical, statistical, and analytical knowledge is necessary that includes training in Machine Learning or Machine Learning (neural networks, ensembles, SVMs, Deep Learning), pattern recognition, predictive models, clustering techniques, Data Mining or Data Mining (mining of texts, images, speech), PLN or Natural Language Processing, Sentiment Analysis, etc.

But for applying Big Data techniques to business to yield the best possible results, in addition to great computing capacity, we must know how to combine storage and processing capacity with analysis capacity. There are three different levels of data analytics:

- Descriptive analytics is used to determine how the business is working.
- Predictive analytics allows for anticipating what will foreseeably happen in the future. At this level, we find algorithm libraries to which the data scientist can resort, such as Scikit-learn, Keras, Tensorflow, nltk
- And finally, prescriptive analytics offers the greatest competitive advantage because its recommendations on the best strategy to achieve the best results allow better-informed decisions. This level, the authoritarian, is the most unexplored. Along with the predictive analytics tools, other tools can be used to solve the optimization component of any prescriptive solution: CPLEX, Gurobi, and Matlab packages…, but building the global solution usually requires specific software development for each project.

Big Data tools to visualize data

Apart from knowing how to store data, process, and analyze it, being an expert in Big Data entails communicating the information that this data, after its classification and study, has provided us. For this, it is essential to paint the data in a familiar and effective context that facilitates interpreting and visualizing them simply and affordably.

There are affordable data visualization tools for developers or designers and less technical personnel on the market. Most have paid and free versions and offer optimized graphics for use on social networks. Among the most popular would be Tableau, Weave, Datawrappper, Gephi, Infogram, Many Eyes, Piktochart, NodeXL, Chartblocks, d3, Thinglink, Axiis, QuickView, and Google Fusion Tables.

In short, achieving better results involves mastering Big Data tools: having qualified professionals in the use of different data storage and processing systems -both traditional and the most current ones derived from the NoSQL world or the Hadoop ecosystem-creating analysis and visualization solutions —accessible both in SaaS mode and directly at the client's premises— and apply the different levels of analytical techniques for the benefit of the client.

SQL And Big Data

How is SQL in big data different from regular SQL? Big data uses distributed computing.

Calculations are distributed among several servers. One database is located on several servers at once. The query result is also calculated simultaneously by several servers. The MapReduce paradigm describes distributed computing algorithms. Let's look at what this affects and how to upgrade your SQL to the big data level.

Warning: This chapter focuses on canonical data processing architectures. Many modern DBMS and frameworks are built on their basis and contain many improvements and improvements. However, the set of optimizations may differ. Therefore, the actual data processing on your project may differ for the better, thanks to your particular tool. It is important to understand exactly what optimizations your framework can perform to control algorithms' effectiveness properly.

Basics of the MapReduce Paradigm

The first thing to remember is that in big data, almost any database stores data on multiple servers.

Let's imagine that we have three servers and a table of clients. The whole table is evenly distributed into three parts, each server stores 1/3 of the data. To return the query result, we need to read each part from each server and collect everything on one server, where we view the result.

The simplest SQL query:

SELECT * FROM CLIENTS

Even such a simple query is broken down into three mandatory parts of MapReduce:

1.   Map

2.   Shuffle

3.   Reduce

Each of these operations is distributed and parallelized differently, so it is important to understand what they are.

- The Map stage is often a simple hard disk read. In addition to reading, one-line transformations and filters can be used here, i.e., operations without join, group by, order by, distinct, and without aggregation functions. Operations at this stage are always well parallelized and do not create a load on the database because each server only reads the data it has on its hard portion drive. The data is often stored uniformly on each server. All servers participate in this stage and share the load evenly.

- At the Shuffle stage, no calculations occur, but all data is moved between servers so that the final result can be obtained from them at the Reduce stage. This step will become clear only after diving into the Reduce stage, so let's move on to it.
- The Reduce stage is the most insidious because it can cause big problems with database performance. All grouping operations take place here, as well as operations that record the result. Some operations cannot run on multiple servers simultaneously, requiring the entire amount of data to be collected on a single server. The request will always fail if the data does not fit on one server.

Let's take a closer look at the examples below.

How to Write Effective SQL Queries

Let's go back to the request:

SELECT * FROM CLIENTS

Here we will get a uniform reading of the Table on three servers. But what to do with the result? If we want to display it on the screen, the result must be collected on a single server from which we execute the request. Our last step of displaying the screen reduces distributed computing to nothing - the final load will fall on our server, where we get the result.

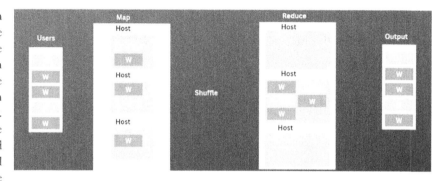

The Map stage will be distributed. Next, the Shuffle stage will follow, transferring all the data to one final server, which will have to accommodate the full result and display it on the screen. If the data is so large that it does not fit on one server, even such a simple query will never be executed. The resulting server will always return an Out of memory error.

MapReduce Model Diagram

This query can be easily changed:

INSERT INTO CLIENTS_NEW SELECT * FROM CLIENTS

Instead of displaying the result on the screen, the result will be written in another table. Since the other Table is also stored and distributed, three servers can write simultaneously.

Thus, collecting all the data in one place will not be necessary, and all calculations will be well distributed. The Map stage will parallelize well, but now the Reduce stage (recording the result) will be distributed

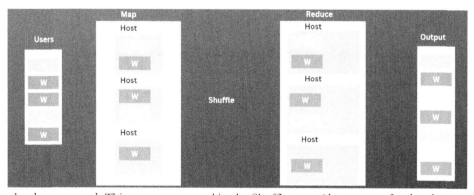

on the same servers where the data was read. This means we can skip the Shuffle stage (do not transfer data between servers before writing the result), which also speeds up calculations.

Data is not collected on one server

Similar logic applies to filter operations like SELECT * FROM CLIENTS WHERE CLIENTS.GENDER = 1and so on. Such filters will also be distributed in the Map stage.

Operations with aggregations

Consider now operations with aggregations. Let's say we want to count the number of customers by gender.

The SQL query is like this:

SELECT COUNT(*) FROM THE CLIENTS GROUP BY CLIENTS.GENDER

Map stage without surprises, again parallel reading by three servers. But Reducing changes everything.

Since we have a grouping by gender, we want to see two numbers in the answer - the number of men and the number of women. This means we can use a maximum of two servers at the Reduce stage. One server should count all men, the other - all women. To do this, at the Shuffle stage, it is necessary to transfer the records of all men to one server and the records of women to another server. Then, at the Reduce stage, the servers will only have to count all the records received at the Shuffle stage.

We can see that Reduce distributes the calculations depending on the grouping functions. This logic applies to all aggregate functions, distinct, join (where the grouping is based on the join condition), and sortings.

At the Shuffle stage, the data is divided according to the specified attribute

With sorting, you need to be especially careful. To sort all records without grouping by key, Reduce will collect all records on one server and sort non-distributed. Therefore, operations performed with uneven grouping (when there are fewer grouping keys than available servers) should be avoided.

Now you know what to look out for when writing big data queries. The key to writing an efficient query is to monitor the consumed database resources as your query changes. Change the order of joins, groupings, and subqueries and look for the best combination of performance/load.

Book 5: SQL Interview

SQL seems to be one of the fastest-growing programming languages, which is amazing because, technically, it is NOT a programming language! How did this happen, and how was it possible? Well, this is exactly what I will explain to you in addition to covering the possible SQL interview questions so that you can get the job of your dreams!

This book will cover interview questions such as what SQL is, Microsoft SQL Server, MySQL, and all those questions a potential employer might ask you, from the basics to the most advanced information. Then, we'll discuss some general things to consider before, during, and after your job interview.

If you're applying for a new DBA job or a job that requires knowledge of databases, you'll probably want to study the most common interview questions. If that is your case, this book may be useful.

Chapter 1: Common SQL Interview Questions and Answers

SQL questions in interviews are common, and to avoid failing, you need to understand better how to work with databases. This list provides the most common SQL interview questions and challenges, along with their answers.

- What is a DBMS?

Let's say there is a large database that many employees use: someone is looking for information, and someone changes or even deletes it. To properly process all these requests, you need special software called a database management system (DBMS).

- What types of DBMS, according to data models, do you know?

This SQL question is not just about naming but also briefly describes each type.

There are several types of DBMS :

- Relational, which supports establishing relationships between tables using primary and foreign keys. An example is MySQL.
- Flat File - databases with two-dimensional files containing records of the same type and no connection to other files, as in relational ones. An example is Excel.
- Hierarchical refers to the existence of records related to each other in a one-to-one or one-to-many relationship. But for many-to-many relationships, you should use the relational model. An example is Adabas.
- Network ones are similar to hierarchical ones, but in this case, a "child" can have several "parents" and vice versa. Examples are IDS and IDMS.
- Object-oriented DBMSs work with databases made up of objects used in OOP. Objects are grouped into classes and are called instances, and classes, in turn, interact through methods. Object An example is Versant.
- -relational models have the advantages of relational and object-oriented models. An example is IBM Db2.
- The multidimensional model is a variation of the relational model and uses multidimensional structures. Often represented as data cubes. An example is Oracle Essbase.
- Hybrid databases consist of two or more types of databases. Used when one type is not enough to handle all requests. An example is Altibase HDB.

- What is a primary key?

The primary key is designed to uniquely identify every record in a table and is strictly unique: no two records in a table can contain the same primary key value. Null values (NULL) in PRIMARY KEY are not allowed. If PRIMARY KEY multiple fields are used as a key, they are called a composite key.

Example:

```
CREATE TABLE USERS (
  id INT NOT NULL,
  name VARCHAR (20) NOT NULL,
  PRIMARY KEY (id)
);
```

Here, the id field is used as the primary key.

- When is PRIMARY KEY used?

PRIMARY KEY links to the child table containing the foreign key.

- What is a foreign key?

The foreign key or FOREIGN KEY is also an attribute of the constraint and provides a relationship between two tables. Essentially, it is a field or multiple fields that are referenced PRIMARY KEY in the parent table.

Usage example:

```
CREATE TABLE order (
  order_id INT NOT NULL,
  user_id INT,
  PRIMARY KEY (order_id),
  FOREIGN KEY (user_id) REFERENCES users(id)
);
```

In this case, the foreign key bound to a field user_id in the table order refers to the primary key id in the table users, and it is on these fields that the two tables are linked.

- What other restrictions do you know, how do they work, and are they indicated?

SQL constraints are specified when creating or modifying a table. These are rules for restricting the type of data stored in a table. The data action will not be performed if the set restrictions are violated.

- UNIQUE- guarantees the uniqueness of the values in the column;
- NOT NULL- value cannot be NULL;
- INDEX- creates indexes in the table for quick searches/queries;
- CHECK— the values of the column must meet the given conditions;
- DEFAULT- provides the column with default values.
- What is the ORDER BY keyword used for?

To sort data in ascending (ASC) or descending (DESC) order.

Usage example:

SELECT * FROM user ORDER BY name DESC;

Users are selected to be sorted by name in descending order. Extend the SQL answer to this question by saying that without the specification, the DESC data would be sorted by default - in ascending order:

SELECT * FROM user ORDER BY name;

- Name the four main join types in SQL

To merge two tables into one, use the JOIN. The table can be inner (INNER) or outer (OUTER), and outer joins can be left (LEFT), right (RIGHT), or full (FULL).

- INNER JOIN- getting records with the same values in both tables, i.e., getting the intersection of tables.
- FULL OUTER JOIN- merges records from both tables (if the join condition is true) and complements them with all records from both tables that do not have matches. The missing field will be NULL for records that do not have matches from another table.
- LEFT JOIN- returns all records that satisfy the join condition, plus all remaining records from the outer (left) table that do not satisfy the join condition.
- RIGHT JOIN- works the same as the left join; only the right one will be used as the external table.

Consider an example of joining SQL tables using INNER JOIN. The following query selects all orders with customer information:

```
SELECT Orders.OrderID, Customers.CustomerName
FROM Orders
INNER JOIN Customers ON Orders.CustomerID = Customers.CustomerID;
```

- What is Self JOIN?

This question can also be asked in a SQL interview. This expression is used to join a table with itself as if it were two different tables. To implement this, one of these "tables" is temporarily renamed.

For example, the following SQL query aggregates customers from the same city:

```
SELECT A.CustomerName AS CustomerName1, B.CustomerName AS CustomerName2, A.City
FROM Customers A, Customers B
WHERE A.CustomerID <> B.CustomerID
AND A.City = B.City
ORDER BY A.City;
```

- What is the UNION operator for?

It combines received data from two or more queries, which must have the same number of columns with the same data types and in the same order.

Usage example:

```
SELECT column(s) FROM first_table
UNION
SELECT column(s) FROM second_table;
```

- How do wildcards work?

These special characters are needed to replace any characters in the query. They are used in conjunction with the operator LIKE, which can filter the requested data.

- What are wildcards?
- %— replace zero or more characters;
- _— replace one character.

Examples:

```
SELECT * FROM user WHERE name LIKE '%test%';
SELECT * FROM user WHERE name LIKE 't_est';
```

This query allows you to find the data of all users whose names contain "test."

And in this case, the names of the users you are looking for begin with "t," then contain some character and "est" at the end.

- What do Aliases do?

SQL aliases give a temporary name to a table or column. This is needed when the query contains tables or columns with ambiguous names. In this case, for convenience, aliases are used in the query. The SQL alias only exists for the duration of the query.

Example:

```
SELECT very_long_column_name AS alias_name
FROM table;
```

- What is the INSERT INTO SELECT statement for?

This statement copies data from one table and pastes it into another, while the data types in both tables must match.

Usage example:

```
INSERT INTO second_table
SELECT * FROM first_table
WHERE condition;
```

- What are normalization and denormalization?

Relationship normalization in SQL is designed to organize the information in the database so that it does not take up much space and is convenient to work with. This is the removal of redundant data, the elimination of duplicates, the identification of related data sets through PRIMARY KEY, etc.

Accordingly, denormalization is the reverse process, introducing redundant data into the normalized table.

- Explain the difference between DELETE and TRUNCATE commands

A command DELETE is a DML operation that removes records from a table that match a given condition:

DELETE FROM table_name WHERE condition;

In this case, deletion logs are created; the operation can be canceled.

But the command TRUNCATE is a DDL operation that completely recreates the table, and it is impossible to undo such a deletion:

TRUNCATE TABLE table_name;

- How is VARCHAR different from NVARCHAR?

The main difference is that VARCHAR stores values in ASCII format, where a character occupies one byte, and NVARCHAR stores values in Unicode format, where a character "weighs" 2 bytes. The type VARCHAR should be used if you are certain the values will not contain Unicode characters. For example, VARCHAR can be applied to e-mail addresses consisting of ASCII characters.

Practice

1. How do you select records with odd Ids?

One of the most common interview questions. The SQL query to select records with odd numbers id should look like this:

SELECT * FROM sample WHERE id % 2 != 0;

If the remainder of the division id by 2 is zero, we have an actual value and vice versa.

2. How to find duplicates in an email field?

```
SELECT email, COUNT(email)
FROM customers
GROUP BY email
HAVING COUNT(email) > 1;
```

The function COUNT()returns the number of rows from the field email. The operator HAVING works almost the same as WHERE, except that it is applied not to all columns but to the set created by the GROUP BY.

3. When selecting from a table, add one day to the date

SELECT DATE_ADD(date, 1 DAY) as new_date FROM table;

The function DATE_ADD()adds a given time to date. The syntax looks like this:

SELECT DATE_ADD(date, INTERVAL add what) FROM table_name WHERE condition;

4. Select unique names

SELECT DISTINCT name FROM users;

SELECT DISTINCT returns different values even if duplicates are in the selected column.

5. Find the average salary of employees in the table

SELECT AVG(salary) FROM workers;

The AVG()only applies to numeric data types and returns the average of the column.

6. And now get a list of employees with above-average salaries

SELECT * FROM workers

WHERE salary > (SELECT AVG (salary) FROM workers);

7. Given tables, workers, and departments. Find all departments without a single employee

```
SELECT department_name
FROM workers w
RIGHT JOIN departments d ON (w.department_id = d.department_id)
WHERE first_name IS NULL;
```

8. Replace the worker's salary in the table with 1000 if it is 900, and with 1500 otherwise

Replacing values is one of the most common SQL tasks in job interviews. Solving it is easy:

```
UPDATE table SET salary =
CASE
WHEN salary = 900 THEN 1000
ELSE 1500
END;
```

The statement UPDATE is used to modify existing entries. But answers to questions like this from interviews in SQL should be more detailed. Specify that after the UPDATE should specify which records should be updated. Otherwise, all records in the table will be updated.

In our example, the condition is specified through the CASE statement: if the current salary is 900, we change it to 1000; in other cases - to 1500.

9. When fetching from the user table, create a field that will include both names and salary

SELECT CONCAT(name, salary) AS new_field FROM users;

The function CONCAT()is used to concatenate (combine) strings, implicitly converting any data types to strings.

10. Rename the table

ALTER TABLE first_table RENAME second_table;

Using the operator ALTER TABLE, you can add, delete, change columns, and change the table's name.

Chapter 2: Technical Interview

The list is based on my own work experience and interview. I tried to select only those questions, the answers that can help in practice and not just in a technical interview. The questions relate to the basic mechanisms of the language; therefore, first of all, they will be of interest to beginners, but perhaps, seasoned developers will learn something new from them. So let's get started.

- What will the condition return 2 <> NULL?

Comparison with NULL is probably the first pitfall people stumble upon when working with a database. Contrary to the usual logic, the condition

2 <> NULL

returns false (FALSE), as well as the condition

2 = NULL

The point here is that the type of value NULL in SQL has a slightly different shade of meaning than in applied programming languages. If in C-like languages \u200b\u200bit NULL means the absence of some value, then in SQL, it means only that we do not know this value. For this reason, any comparison with NULL returns false.

Returning to the essence of the matter, we cannot say, "Two is not equal NULL" Because we do not know the value to the right of the inequality sign, and there might be a two.

- What will the condition return 3 NOT IN (1, 2, NULL)?

Here is the same story as in the previous case. Condition

3 NOT IN (1, 2, NULL)

returns false (FALSE), like the condition

3 IN (1, 2, NULL)

The reason for this lies in the peculiarities of the operator IN operation. When checking that a particular value is in the collection, the operator IN simply compares that value with each element in the collection.

In other words:

3 IN (1, 2, NULL)

it's the same as

(3 = 1) OR (3 = 2) OR (3 = NULL)

In case of NOT IN condition:

3 NOT IN (1, 2, NULL)

it's the same as

(3 <> 1) AND (3 <> 2) AND (3 <> NULL)

As we know from the previous example, it 3 <> NULLreturns false, and hence the whole condition

(3 <> 1) AND (3 <> 2) AND (3 <> NULL)

will also be false.

- Will this request succeed?

```
SELECT
        order_id,
        order_code,
        SUM (order_value)
FROM
        orders
GROUP BY
        order_id
```

There is no single correct answer to this question - it depends on the database. The problem with this query is that the column order_code is not specified in the expression GROUP BY, nor has an aggregate function defined for it. With a column, order_code, we do not know whether to group it or by it.

If this query is run in MySQL, then the column order_codewill be added to the expression GROUP BY automatically, and the query will run normally. An error will be generated by default if MS SQL Server executes this query. However, this behavior is configurable.

- Why won't this query run?

```
SELECT
        username,
        YEAR (user_birth_date) AS year_of_birth
FROM
        users
WHERE
        year_of_birth = 2000
```

The query will fail due to an alias reference year_of_birth in the expression WHERE. The fact is that field aliases in SQL are used to format data already received from the database. Therefore, they can only be used in expressions responsible for formatting the result, such as GROUP BY, ORDER, BY, and HAVING. In expressions responsible for receiving data, such as WHERE you must use the original field names.

```
WHERE
        YEAR (user_birth_date) = 2000
```

- Does the order of columns in a composite index matter?

Yes.

```
CREATE NONCLUSTERED INDEX MyInd on users (user_name, user_birth_date);
```

It's not the same as

```
CREATE NONCLUSTERED INDEX MyInd on users (user_birth_date, user_name);
```

When creating a composite index, first, a regular index is built for its first column, then an index for the second column is built based on it, and so on.

In other words, the most frequently searched columns should be listed first in the composite index.

- What is the difference between the types CHAR and VARCHAR?

Both of these types are used to store textual information of limited length, and the differences between them are as follows:

- 1. The type CHAR stores a fixed length value. If a string placed in a column of this type is shorter than the length of the type, the string will be padded with spaces. CHAR(10)For example, if you write a string to a type column, it will be saved as SQL.
- The type VARCHAR stores a value of variable length. Each value of this type is allocated as much memory as is needed for that particular value.
- 2. CHAR type uses static memory allocation, making operations faster than VARCHAR.

Thus, the type is suitable for storing fixed-length string data (for example, inventory numbers and hashes), and for other strings, CHAR is more suitable.VARCHARNVARCHAR

- What is the difference between types VARCHAR and NVARCHAR?

NVARCHAR is perhaps the most versatile of the string data types in a database. It allows you to store variable-length strings in Unicode format. Each character takes 2 bytes in this format, and the encoding contains 65,536 characters and includes all world languages, including hieroglyphs.

The type VARCHAR stores data in SACII format. Each character occupies 1 byte in this format, but the individual encoding contains only 256 characters. Because of this, each world language has its encoding.

Thus, it is VARCHAR worth storing string data in a format that does not need to be translated (for example, email addresses). For other cases, it is more suitable NVARCHAR.

- What is the difference between UNION and UNION ALL?

Expressions UNION and UNION ALL are very reliable providers of extra or missing rows in the result of a query. Both of these expressions are used to combine the results of multiple independent queries. And the difference between them is that if there are identical rows in the query results, UNION will remove duplicates, leaving only one of such rows. At the same time, UNION ALL, as you might guess from the name, will merge the results of queries, ignoring duplicates.

- What is the difference between the expressions WHERE and HAVING?

And finally, the question that is asked in almost every database interview: is about HAVING.

Expressions WHEREand HAVINGare used to filter the result of a query and expect some condition after them, according to which the data needs to be filtered. But, if it WHEREworks on its own and filters the data of each row of the result separately, then the expression HAVING makes sense only in combination with the expression GROUP BY and filters already grouped values.

Chapter 3: Advance level Interview Guide

You need to understand that interviews for data analysts and data scientists ask questions not only about SQL. Other common topics include past project discussions, A/B testing, metrics development, and open analytics issues. About three years ago, Quora posted interview tips for a Facebook product analyst position. This topic is discussed in more detail there. However, if improving your knowledge of SQL will help you in the interview, this guide is well worth the time.

Percent change from month to month

Context: It's often useful to know how a key metric changes monthly, like monthly active users. Let's say we have a table login like this:

```
| user_id | date |
|---------|------------|
| 1 | 2018-07-01 |
| 234 | 2018-07-02 |
| 3 | 2018-07-02 |
| 1 | 2018-07-02 |
| ... | ... |
| 234 | 2018-10-04 |
```

Task: Find the monthly percentage change in active users (MAU).

Solution:

(This solution, like other blocks of code in this document, contains comments about SQL syntax elements that may differ between different SQL variants and other notes)

```sql
WITH mau AS
(
  SELECT
  /*
  * Usually the interviewer will let you write pseudocode for
    * date functions, i.e. will NOT check if you remember them.
    * Simply explain on the board what the function does
    *
    * DATE_TRUNC() is available in Postgres, but similar result
    * may give other SQL date functions or combinations thereof
    */
    DATE_TRUNC('month', date) month_timestamp,
    COUNT(DISTINCT user_id) mau
  FROM
    logins
  GROUP BY
    DATE_TRUNC('month', date)
)

SELECT
  /*
  * This SELECT statement does not need to literally include the previous month.
  *
  * But as mentioned in the tips section above, it can be helpful
  * at least sketch out self-joins so as not to get confused which
  * the table represents the last month to the current month, and so on.
  */
  a.month_timestamp previous_month,
  a.mau previous_mau,
  b.month_timestamp current_month,
  b.mau current_mau,
  ROUND(100.0*(b.mau - a.mau)/a.mau,2) AS percent_change
FROM
  mau a
JOIN
  /*
  * Alternatively `ON b.month_timestamp = a.month_timestamp + interval '1 month'`
  */
  mau b ON a.month_timestamp = b.month_timestamp - interval '1 month'
```

Tree Structure Labeling

Context: Let's say you have a table tree with two columns: the first lists the nodes, and the second lists the parent nodes.

node parent
1 2
2 5
3 5
4 3
5 NULL

Goal: write SQL in such a way that we designate each node as inner (inner), root (root), or leaf node (leaf) so that for the above values, the following will turn out:

node	label
1	Leaf
2	Inner
3	Inner
4	Leaf
5	Root

(Note: You can read more about tree data structure terminology here. However, it's not needed to solve this problem!)

```
WITH join_table AS
(
  SELECT
    cur.node,
    cur.parent,
    COUNT(next.node) AS num_children
  FROM
    tree cur
  LEFT JOIN
    tree next ON (next.parent = cur.node)
  GROUP BY
    cur.node,
    cur.parent
)
SELECT
  node,
  CASE
    WHEN parent IS NULL THEN "Root"
    WHEN num_children = 0 THEN "Leaf"
    ELSE "Inner"
  END AS label
FROM
  join_table
```

An alternate solution, no explicit joins: a condition is required for WHERE parent IS NOT NULLthis solution is to return Leaf instead of NULL.

```
SELECT
  node,
  CASE
    WHEN parent IS NULL THEN 'Root'
    WHEN node NOT IN
      (SELECT parent FROM tree WHERE parent IS NOT NULL) THEN 'Leaf'
    WHEN node IN (SELECT parent FROM tree) AND parent IS NOT NULL THEN 'Inner'
  END AS label
from
  tree
```

User retention per month (multiple parts)

Context: let's say we have statistics on user authorization on the site in the table logins:

```
| user_id | date       |
|---------|------------|
| 1       | 2018-07-01 |
| 234     | 2018-07-02 |
| 3       | 2018-07-02 |
| 1       | 2018-07-02 |
| ...     | ...        |
| 234     | 2018-10-04 |
```

Task: write a query that gets the number of retained users per month. In our case, this parameter is defined as the number of users who logged into the system both in this and in the previous month.

Decision:

```
SELECT
  DATE_TRUNC('month', a.date) month_timestamp,
  COUNT(DISTINCT a.user_id) retained_users
FROM
  logins a
JOIN
  logins b ON a.user_id = b.user_id
    AND DATE_TRUNC('month', a.date) = DATE_TRUNC('month', b.date) +
                  interval '1 month'
GROUP BY
  date_trunc('month', a.date)
```

Pre-deduplicating the user_id before self-joining makes the solution more efficient, and suggested the code below.

Alternative solution:

```
WITH DistinctMonthlyUsers AS (
/*
  * For each month, we define a *set* of users who
  * completed authorization
  */
  SELECT DISTINCT
    DATE_TRUNC('MONTH', a.date) AS month_timestamp,
    user_id
  FROM logins
)

SELECT
  CurrentMonth.month_timestamp month_timestamp,
  COUNT(PriorMonth.user_id) AS retained_user_count
FROM
  DistinctMonthlyUsers AS CurrentMonth
LEFT JOIN
  DistinctMonthlyUsers AS PriorMonth
ON
  CurrentMonth.month_timestamp = PriorMonth.month_timestamp + INTERVAL '1 MONTH'
  AND
  CurrentMonth.user_id = PriorMonth.user_id
```

Challenge: Now let's take the previous problem of calculating the number of retained users per month - and turn it on its head. Let's write a query to count users who did not return to the site this month. That is, "lost" users.

Decision:

```
SELECT
  DATE_TRUNC('month', a.date) month_timestamp,
  COUNT(DISTINCT b.user_id) churned_users
FROM
  logins a
FULL OUTER JOIN
  logins b ON a.user_id = b.user_id
    AND DATE_TRUNC('month', a.date) = DATE_TRUNC('month', b.date) +
                        interval '1 month'
WHERE
  a.user_id IS NULL
GROUP BY
  DATE_TRUNC('month', a.date)
```

user_id	month_date
1	2018-05-01
234	2018-05-01
3	2018-05-01
12	2018-05-01
...	...
234	2018-10-01

This problem can also be solved using joins LEFT or RIGHT.

Note: this is probably a more difficult task than you will be in a real interview. Treat it more like a puzzle, or skip it and move on to the next problem.

Context: So we've done well with the previous two problems. Under the new task's terms, we now have a table of lost user_churns. If the user was active last month but not this month, he is entered in the table for this month. Here's what it looks like user_churns:

Challenge: Now, you want to do a cohort analysis, that is, an analysis of the population of active users who have been reactivated in the past. Create a table with such users. You can use tables user_churnsand to create cohort logins. In Postgres, the current timestamp is available via current_timestamp.

Decision:

```
WITH user_login_data AS
(
    SELECT
        DATE_TRUNC('month', a.date) month_timestamp,
        a.user_id,
        /*
        * At least in the SQL variants I've used,
         * no need to include columns from HAVING in the SELECT statement.
         * I wrote them out here for clarity.
         */
        MAX(b.month_date) as most_recent_churn,
        MAX(DATE_TRUNC('month', c.date)) as most_recent_active
    FROM
        logins a
    JOIN
        user_churns b
            ON a.user_id = b.user_id AND DATE_TRUNC('month', a.date) > b.month_date
    JOIN
        logins c
            ON a.user_id = c.user_id
            AND
            DATE_TRUNC('month', a.date) > DATE_TRUNC('month', c.date)
    WHERE
        DATE_TRUNC('month', a.date) = DATE_TRUNC('month', current_timestamp)
    GROUP BY
        DATE_TRUNC('month', a.date),
        a.user_id
    HAVING
        most_recent_churn > most_recent_active
```

Cumulative Total

Context: Let's say we have a table of transactions like this:

date	cash_flow
2018-01-01	-1000
2018-01-02	-100
2018-01-03	50
...	...

Where cash_flow is the revenue minus the costs for each day.

Task: write a query to get the running total for the cash flow each day in such a way that you end up with a table in the following form:

date	cumulative_cf
2018-01-01	-1000
2018-01-02	-1100
2018-01-03	-1050
...	...

Decision:

```
SELECT
    a.date date,
    SUM(b.cash_flow) as cumulative_cf
FROM
    transactions a
JOIN b
    transactions b ON a.date >= b.date
GROUP BY
    a.date
ORDER BY
    date ASC
```

An alternative solution using the window function (more efficient!):

```
SELECT
    date,
    SUM(cash_flow) OVER (ORDER BY date ASC) as cumulative_cf
FROM
    transactions
ORDER BY
    date ASC
```

Moving Average

Note: The moving average can be calculated in different ways. Here we use the previous average. Thus, the metric for the seventh day of the month will be the average of the previous six days and itself.

Context: Let's say we have a table signup like this:

Task: write a query to get a 7-day moving average of daily signups.

date	sign_ups
2018-01-01	10
2018-01-02	20
2018-01-03	50
...	...
2018-10-01	35

Decision:

```
SELECT
    a.date,
    AVG(b.sign_ups) average_sign_ups
FROM
    signups a
JOIN
    signups b ON a.date <= b.date + interval '6 days' AND a.date >= b.date
GROUP BY
    a.date
```

Multiple Connection Conditions

Context: Let's say our table email contains emails sent from zach@g.comand received to an address:

```
| id | subject | from | to | timestamp |
|----|----------|--------------|--------------|--------------------|
| 1 | Yosemite | zach@g.com | thomas@g.com | 2018-01-02 12:45:03 |
| 2 | Big Sur | sarah@g.com | thomas@g.com | 2018-01-02 16:30:01 |
| 3 | Yosemite | thomas@g.com | zach@g.com | 2018-01-02 16:35:04 |
| 4 | running | jill@g.com | zach@g.com | 2018-01-03 08:12:45 |
| 5 | Yosemite | zach@g.com | thomas@g.com | 2018-01-03 14:02:01 |
| 6 | Yosemite | thomas@g.com | zach@g.com | 2018-01-03 15:01:05 |
| .. | .. | .. | .. | .. |
```

Task: write a query to get the response time for each email (id) sent to zach@g.com. Do not include letters to other addresses. Let's assume that each thread has a unique topic. Remember that a thread can have multiple emails back and forth between zach@g.com and other recipients.

Decision:

```
SELECT
    a.id,
    MIN(b.timestamp) - a.timestamp as time_to_respond
FROM
    emails a
JOIN
    emails b
        ON
            b.subject = a.subject
        AND
            a.to = b.from
        AND
            a.from = b.to
        AND
            a.timestamp < b.timestamp
WHERE
    a.to = 'zach@g.com'
GROUP BY
    a.id
```

Tasks for window functions

- Find the id with the maximum value

Context: Let's say we have a table of salaries with data about departments and salaries of employees in the following format:

Task: write a request to get empnothe highest salary. Make sure your solution handles cases of equal salaries!

```
depname | empno | salary |
---+-------+--------+
develop | 11 | 5200 |
develop | 7 | 4200 |
develop | 9 | 4500 |
develop | 8 | 6000 |
develop | 10 | 5200 |
personnel | 5 | 3500 |
personnel | 2 | 3900 |
sales | 3 | 4800 |
sales | 1 | 5000 |
sales | 4 | 4800 |
```

Decision:

```
WITH max_salary AS (
  SELECT
    MAX(salary) max_salary
  FROM
    salaries
  )
SELECT
  s.empno
FROM
  salaries s
JOIN
  max_salary ms ON s.salary = ms.max_salary
```

Alternative solution using RANK():

```
WITH sal_rank AS
  (SELECT
    empno,
    RANK() OVER(ORDER BY salary DESC) rnk
  FROM
    salaries)
SELECT
  empno
FROM
  sal_rank
WHERE
  rnk = 1;
```

- Mean and Ranking with a Window Function (Multiple Parts)

Context: Let's say we have a table of salaries in this format:

```
depname | empno | salary |
---+-------+--------+
develop | 11 | 5200 |
develop | 7 | 4200 |
develop | 9 | 4500 |
develop | 8 | 6000 |
develop | 10 | 5200 |
personnel | 5 | 3500 |
personnel | 2 | 3900 |
sales | 3 | 4800 |
sales | 1 | 5000 |
sales | 4 | 4800 |
```

Challenge: Write a query that returns the same table but with a new column that lists the average salary for the department. We would expect a table like this:

```
depname | empno | salary | avg_salary |
---+-------+--------+------------+
develop | 11 | 5200 | 5020 |
develop | 7 | 4200 | 5020 |
develop | 9 | 4500 | 5020 |
develop | 8 | 6000 | 5020 |
develop | 10 | 5200 | 5020 |
personnel | 5 | 3500 | 3700 |
personnel | 2 | 3900 | 3700 |
sales | 3 | 4800 | 4867 |
sales | 1 | 5000 | 4867 |
sales | 4 | 4800 | 4867 |
```

Decision:

```
SELECT
  *,
  /*
  * AVG() is a Postgres command, but other SQL flavors like BigQuery use
  * AVERAGE()
  */
  ROUND(AVG(salary),0) OVER (PARTITION BY depname) avg_salary
FROM
  salaries
```

Challenge: Write a query that adds a column with each employee's position in the time sheet based on their salary in their department, where the employee with the highest salary gets the position. We would expect a table like this:

```
depname | empno | salary | salary_rank |
---+-------+--------+-------------+

develop | 11 | 5200 | 2 |
develop | 7 | 4200 | 5 |
develop | 9 | 4500 | 4 |
develop | 8 | 6000 | 1 |
develop | 10 | 5200 | 2 |
personnel | 5 | 3500 | 2 |
personnel | 2 | 3900 | 1 |
sales | 3 | 4800 | 2 |
sales | 1 | 5000 | 1 |
sales | 4 | 4800 | 2 |
```

Decision:

```
SELECT
  *,
  RANK() OVER(PARTITION BY depname ORDER BY salary DESC) salary_rank
FROM
  salaries
```

Other tasks of medium and high complexity

- Histograms

Context: Let's say we have a table session where each row represents a video streaming session with a length in seconds:

```
| session_id | length_seconds |
|------------------|----------------|
| 1 | 23 |
| 2 | 453 |
| 3 | 27 |
| .. | .. |
```

Task: write a query to count the number of sessions that fall in intervals of five seconds, i.e., for the snippet above, the result will be something like this:

The maximum score counts for proper line labels ("5-10", etc.)

```
| bucket | count |
|---------|-------|
| 20-25 | 2 |
| 450-455 | 1 |
```

Solution:

```
WITH bin_label AS
(SELECT
   session_id,
   FLOOR(length_seconds/5) as bin_label
FROM
   sessions
)
SELECT
   CONCATENTATE(STR(bin_label*5), '-', STR(bin_label*5+5)) bucket,
   COUNT(DISTINCT session_id) count
GROUP BY
   bin_label
ORDER BY
   bin_label ASC
```

Cross connection (multiple parts)

Context: Let's say we have a table state_streamswhere each row contains the name of the state and the total hours of streaming from the video host:

state	total_streams
NC	34569
SC	33999
ca	98324
MA	19345
..	..

(Actually, this type of aggregated table usually has a date column, but for this task, we will exclude it)

Task: write a query to get pairs of states with a total number of threads within a thousand of each other. For the snippet above, we would like to see something like this:

state_a	state_b
NC	SC
SC	NC

Decision:

```
SELECT
   a.state as state_a,
   b.state as state_b
FROM
   state_streams a
CROSS JOIN
   state_streams b
WHERE
   ABS(a.total_streams - b.total_streams) < 1000
   AND
   a.state <> b.state
```

For information, cross joins can also be written without explicitly specifying a join:

```
SELECT
    a.state as state_a,
    b.state as state_b
FROM
    state_streams a, state_streams b
WHERE
    ABS(a.total_streams - b.total_streams) < 1000
    AND
    a.state <> b.state
```

Challenge: How can the SQL from the previous solution be modified to remove duplicates? For example, in the same table, NC and SC appear only once, not twice.

Decision:

```
SELECT
    a.state as state_a,
    b.state as state_b
FROM
    state_streams a, state_streams b
WHERE
    ABS(a.total_streams - b.total_streams) < 1000
    AND
    a.state > b.state
```

Advanced Calculations

Note: this is probably a more difficult task than you will be in a real interview. Treat it more like a puzzle - or you can skip it!

Context: let's say we have a table of this kind, where different values of the class can correspond to the same user: user class

user	class
1	a
1	b
1	b
2	b
3	a

Challenge: Suppose there are only two possible values for a class. Write a query to count the number of users in each class. In this case, users with both labels a and b must belong to class b.

For our example, this will be the result:

class	count
a	1
b	2

Decision:

```
WITH usr_b_sum AS
(
  SELECT
    user,
    SUM(CASE WHEN class = 'b' THEN 1 ELSE 0 END) num_b
  FROM
    table
  GROUP BY
    user
),
usr_class_label AS
(
  SELECT
    user,
    CASE WHEN num_b > 0 THEN 'b' ELSE 'a' END class
  FROM
    usr_b_sum
)
SELECT
  class,
  COUNT(DISTINCT user) count
FROM
  usr_class_label
GROUP BY
  class
ORDER BY
  class ASC
```

An alternative solution uses the instructions in the SELECT operators: SELECTUNION

```
SELECT
  "a" class,
  COUNT(DISTINCT user_id) -
    (SELECT COUNT(DISTINCT user_id) FROM table WHERE class = 'b') count
UNION
SELECT
  "b" class,
  (SELECT COUNT(DISTINCT user_id) FROM table WHERE class = 'b') count
```

Chapter 4: Tips for Solving Tough Problems in SQL Interviews

First, the standard tips for all coding interviews:

1. Listen carefully to the description of the problem, repeat the essence of the problem to the interviewer
2. Formulate a corner case to demonstrate that you understand the problem (i.e., a string that will not be included in the final SQL query you are about to write)
3. (If the problem is self-joining) For your benefit, draw what a self-join would look like - usually at least three columns: the desired column from the main table, the column to join from the main table, and the column to join from the secondary table: Or, when you are more comfortable with self-join tasks, you can explain this step verbally
4. Start writing SQL, albeit with errors, instead of trying to understand the problem fully. Formulate your assumptions as you go so your interviewer can correct you.

We're not going to talk about " sleep well " or " appearance " again. No, these are common sense questions for most of us - everyone knows that for a formal interview, it is better not to wear shorts, right?

In sports circles, there are special methods of training before competitions. The closer it is, the shorter the duration of the workout, but the intensity increases. You will train for less time but put in more effort during this time.

This approach is ideal not only for sports but also for interviews or preparing for exams. The closer the interview, the less time you should spend studying, but your concentration should be at the maximum. This means you should not be doing extraneous things, taking long breaks, or being distracted. This will help you reduce your pre-interview stress without losing your confidence.

Incidentally, confidence is another topic of discussion. Try to be confident and look confident. There is a definite difference between what you say about your experience in the field of programming and what you behave like the best programmer in the world.

Remember - you can not achieve much in just a couple of days. Of course, there will be interviews where you fail, but you shouldn't think of it as just a bad experience - the more interviews you have, the more experienced you become (learn more interesting SQL problems).

Conclusion:

It's no secret that good programmers are in demand now more than ever. Potential employers are willing to pay huge sums to those who can prove their programming skills and knowledge.

SQL is one of the most popular programming languages. People appreciate the simplicity of the language and the possibilities of its application in various fields. It's fairly easy to learn, but it opens up many possibilities for those who become proficient with it.

Returning to the topic of our guide, there are various SQL tasks and questions that you may encounter in an interview. In this guide, we have covered only a few of them - and this is just the tip of the iceberg. If you are serious about getting a job in this field, you should find gaps in your knowledge and try eliminating them.

We have tried to cover basic and advanced questions that will help you test your knowledge. Moreover, you know the ideal method for preparing for a future interview.

We hope this guide was informative for you and that you use this knowledge wisely.

Book 6: SQL Hands-on Projects

Embracing SQL knowledge and skills is one thing, but convincing a recruiter that you are making a great find is another. And since it's impossible to get into data science without hands-on experience, you need more than "SQL: self-taught" on your resume to improve your career prospects.

Most interviews include a SQL task to determine your ability and comfort level. The best way to get productive SQL experience is to work on examples that mimic real-world scenarios.

By simulating real-life problem situations, case studies help you find SQL-based solutions to real-world problems you may encounter in your workplace in the future.

You can also go to the mode where you get to the SQL editor to solve case studies in real-time. It includes other free online SQL editing applications that you can access to solve your case studies. Studio beekeeper ٤, Squirrel SQL, and so on. Check out How to set up your mail server on a Windows PC.

If you already have a working knowledge of SQL, the best way to increase confidence is to practice. This book contains various exercises for you to polish your SQL skills. Use your knowledge of SQL for a trial run. You can take advantage of these "SQL playgrounds" to your advantage.

You'll also find many great SQL resources and frameworks, so make the most of them.

Chapter 1: SQL Exercises

1. For airlines whose planes have made at least one flight, calculate, to the nearest two decimal places, the average time the planes have been in the air (in minutes). Also, calculate the specified characteristics for all aircraft flown (use the word 'TOTAL').

Output: company, arithmetic mean, geometric mean, mean square, harmonic mean.

```
With t as
(Select ID_comp, convert(numeric(18,2), Case when time_in >= time_out
    Then datediff(minute, time_out, time_in)
    Else datediff(minute, time_out, dateadd(day, 1, time_in))
    End) as trmin
From (Select trip_no
From Pass_in_trip
Group by trip_no, [date]) pt join Trip t on pt.trip_no = t.trip_no
)

Select Coalesce(c.name, 'TOTAL'), A_mean, G_mean, Q_mean, H_mean
From (
Select Id_comp ,
    convert(numeric(18,2), avg(trmin)) A_mean,
    convert(numeric(18,2), Exp(avg(Log(trmin)))) G_mean,
    convert(numeric(18,2), sqrt(avg(trmin*trmin))) Q_mean,  convert(numeric(18,2), count(*)/sum(1/trmin)) H_mean From t  Group by ID_comp  with cube) as a left join Company c on a .ID_comp = c.ID_comp
```

Group all colors by day, month, and year. Each group ID must be in the form "yyyy" for the year, "yyyy-mm" for the month, and "yyyy-mm-dd" for the day.

Output only those groups where the number of times (b_datetime) when the painting was performed is more than 10.

Output: group ID, the total amount of paint spent.

The election of the Director of the PFAN Museum is held only in leap years, on the first Tuesday of April after the first Monday of April.

For each date from the Battles table, determine the date of the next (after this date) election of the Director of the PFAN museum. Conclusion: battle, battle date, election date. Dates should be output in the format "yyyy-mm-dd."

```
Select name, convert(char(10),date,120) as battle_dt
,convert(char(10),MIN(Dateadd(dd,1,dt)),120) as election_dt
From
(Select name, date, Dateadd(yy ,p,Dateadd(dd,n,Dateadd(mm,3,dateadd(yy,datediff(yy,0,date),0)))) as dt
From Battles
,(values(0),(1),(2 ),(3),(4),(5),(6),(7),(8)) T(p)
,(values(0),(1),(2),(3),( 4),(5),(6)) W(n) ) X
Where date<=dt and (Year(dt)%4=0 and Year(dt)%100> 0 or Year(dt)%400=0 )
and DATEPART(dw,dt)=DATEPART(dw,'20140106')
GROUP BY name, date
```

2. Using the Classes table for each country, find the maximum value among the three expressions: numguns*5000, bore*3000, displacement.

Output in three columns:

- country;
- maximum value;
- The word `numguns` - if the maximum is reached for numguns*5000, the word `bore` - if the maximum is reached for bore*3000, the word `displacement` - if the maximum is reached for displacement.

Comment. Print each on a separate line if the maximum is reached for several expressions.

```
Select top 1 with ties country, x, n
 from classes
cross apply(values(numguns*5000,'numguns')
          ,(bore*3000,'bore')
          ,(displacement,'displacement'))V(x,n)
group by country, x, n
order by rank()over(partition by country order by x desc)
```

Assuming that each color lasts exactly one second, determine continuous time intervals with a more than 1-second duration from the utB table.

Output: the date of the first color in the interval, the date of the last color in the interval.

Consider isosceles trapezoids, each of which can be inscribed with a circle touching all sides. In addition, each side has an integer length from the set of b_vol values.

```
SELECT MIN(D)start, MAX(D)finish
FROM
(
SELECT D, SUM(F)OVER(ORDER BY D ROWS UNBOUNDED PRECEDING)F
FROM
(
SELECT B_DATETIME D, IIF(IsNull(DATEDIFF(second, LAG(B_DATETIME)OVER (ORDER BY B_DATETIME), B_DATETIME),0)<=1,0,1)F
FROM utB
)q
)q
GROUP BY F
HAVING DATEDIFF(second,MIN(D),MAX(D))> 0
```

Display the result in 4 columns: Up, Down, Side, and Rad. Here Up is the smaller base, Down is the larger base, Side is the lengths of the sides, and Rad is the radius of the inscribed circle (with two decimal places).

```
select distinct Up=u.b_vol, Down=d.b_vol, Side=s.b_vol,
Rad=cast(POWER((POWER(s.b_vol,2)-POWER((1.*d.b_vol-1.*u .b_vol)/2,2)),1./2.)/2 as dec(15,2))
 from utB u, utB d, utB s
 where u.b_vol<d.b_vol and 1.*u.b_vol +1.*d.b_vol=2.*s.b_vol
```

Consider isosceles trapezoids, each of which can be inscribed with a circle touching all sides. In addition, each side has an integer length from the set of b_vol values.

Display the result in 4 columns: Up, Down, Side, and Rad. Here Up is the smaller base, Down is the larger base, Side is the lengths of the sides,

```
select distinct Up=u.b_vol, Down=d.b_vol, Side=s.b_vol,
Rad=cast(POWER((POWER(s.b_vol,2)-POWER((1.*d.b_vol-1.*u .b_vol)/2,2)),1./2.)/2 as dec(15,2))
 from utB u, utB d, utB s
 where u.b_vol<d.b_vol and 1.*u.b_vol +1.*d.b_vol=2.*s.b_vol
```

and Rad is the radius of the inscribed circle (with two decimal places).

3. Determine the names of different passengers who, more often than others, had to fly to the same place.

Conclusion: name and number of flights at the same place.

```
WITH b AS
(SELECT ID_psg, COUNT(*) as cnt FROM Pass_In_Trip GROUP BY ID_psg, place),
b1 AS
(SELECT DISTINCT ID_psg, cnt FROM b WHERE cnt =(SELECT MAX(cnt) FROM b))
SELECT name, cnt FROM b1 JOIN Passenger p ON (b1.ID_psg = p.ID_psg)
```

4. How much of each piece of paint will it take to paint all non-white squares white?

Conclusion: the amount of each paint is in order (R, G, B)

```
SELECT sum(255-ISNULL ([R],0) ) R , sum(255-isnull([G],0)) G, sum(255-isnull([B],0)) B
FROM
(
/*merging all tables to find paint filling and color for all squares*/
select ISNULL(B_Q_ID, Q_ID) ID, V_COLOR, B_VOL Vol from
utB RIGHT JOIN utQ on B_Q_ID=Q_ID
LEFT JOIN utV on B_V_ID=V_ID
) as SourceT
PIVOT
(
/*rotating table and calculating each paint volume for each square*/
SUM(Vol) For V_COLOR IN ([R], [G], [B])
) Pvt
/*excluding white squares*/
where ISNULL ([R],0) + isnull([G],0) + isnull( [B],0) <765
```

5. What is the maximum number of black squares that could be painted white with the remaining paint?

```
select min(Qty) from (select SUM(RemainPaint)/255 Qty FROM (select V_COLOR, V_ID,
CASE
WHEN SUM(B_VOL) IS NULL
THEN 255
ELSE 255-SUM(B_VOL)
END RemainPaint
from utB right join utV on B_V_ID = V_ID
group by V_COLOR, V_ID
) R
group by V_COLOR
) Q
```

6. Find NOT white and NOT black squares painted with different colors in the ratio 1:1:1.

```
select B_Q_ID, sum(vol)/3 vol
from
(select B_Q_ID, V_COLOR, sum(B_VOL) vol
from utB, utV
where B_V_ID=V_ID
group by B_Q_ID, V_COLOR
) z
group by B_Q_ID
having count(v_color)=3
    and sum( vol)<765
    and sum(vol) % 3=0
```

Chapter 2: Extracting Data from Tables

1. Write an SQL statement to display all the information of all sellers.

```
salesman_id | name | city | commission
-------------+------------+----------+------------
       5001 | James Hoog | new york | 0.15
       5002 | Nail Knite | Paris | 0.13
       5005 | Pit Alex | London | 0.11
       5006 | Mc Lyon | Paris | 0.14
       5007 | Paul Adam | Rome | 0.13
       5003 | Lauson Hen | San Jose | 0.12
```

Solution example:

SELECT * FROM salesman;

Query output:

seller_id name city commission

5001 James Hug New York 0.15

5002 Nail Knite Paris 0.13

5005 Pit Alex London 0.11

5006 Mac Lyon Paris 0.14

5007 Paul Adam Rome 0.13

5003 Lauzon Hen San Jose 0.12

SQL syntax:

```
SELECT [DISTINCT] [<qualifier>.] <ColumnName> | * |
<Expression>
[AS <column_alias>], ...
FROM <table_or_view_name> |
<inline_view>
[[AS]<table_alias>]
[WHERE <predicate>]
[GROUP BY [<qualifier>.] <Column name>, ...
[HAS <predicate>]
]
[ORDER_BY <column_name> |
<Column_number>
[ASC | DESC], ...
];
```

Note. Use * to get a complete list of columns from a table.

Alternative command:

SELECT salesman_id, name, city, commission

2. Write a query that will retrieve the value of the seller id of all sellers, getting orders from customers in the orders table without repeats.

```
ord_no purchase_amt ord_date customer_id salesman_id
---------- ---------- ---------- ----------- --------- --
70001 150.5 2012-10-05 3005 5002
70009 270.65 2012-09-10 3001 5005
70002 65.26 2012-10-05 3002 5001
70004 110.5 2012-08-17 3009 5003
70007 948.5 2012-09-10 3005 5002
70005 2400.6 2012-07-27 3007 5001
70008 5760 2012-09-10 3002 5001
70010 1983.43 2012-10-10 3004 5006
70003 2480.4 2012-10-10 3009 5003
70012 250.45 2012-06-27 3008 5002
70011 75.29 2012-08-17 3003 5007
70013 3045.6 2012-04-25 3002 5001
```

Solution example:

```
SELECT DISTINCT salesman_id
FROM orders;
```

Query output:

```
salesman_id
5002
5003
5006
5001
5005
5007
```

3. Write a query to display the names and cities of a seller that belongs to the city of Paris.

```
salesman_id | name | city | commission
-------------+------------+----------+------------
       5001 | James Hoog | new york | 0.15
       5002 | Nail Knite | Paris | 0.13
       5005 | Pit Alex | London | 0.11
       5006 | Mc Lyon | Paris | 0.14
       5007 | Paul Adam | Rome | 0.13
       5003 | Lauson Hen | San Jose | 0.12
```

Solution example:

```
SELECT name,city
FROM salesman
WHERE city='Paris';
```

Query output:

```
city name
Nail Knite Paris
Mc Lyon Paris
```

4. Write an SQL statement to display all information for customers with a score of 200.

```
customer_id | custom_name | city | grade | salesman_id
-------------+----------------+------------+------ -+-------------
    3002 | Nick Rimando | new york | 100 | 5001
    3007 | Brad Davis | new york | 200 | 5001
    3005 | Graham Zusi | California | 200 | 5002
    3008 | Julian Green | London | 300 | 5002
    3004 | Fabian Johnson | Paris | 300 | 5006
    3009 | Geoff Cameron | Berlin | 100 | 5003
    3003 | Jozy Altidor | Moscow | 200 | 5007
    3001 | Brad Guzan | London | | 5005
```

Solution example:

```
SELECT *FROM customer
WHERE grade=200;
```

Query output:

```
customer_id cust_name city rating seller_id
3007 Brad Davis NY 200 5001
3005 Graham Zusi California 200 5002
3003 Josi Altidore Moscow 200 5007
```

5. Write an SQL query to display the order number followed by the date of the order and the purchase amount for each order that the seller will deliver with ID 5001.

```
ord_no purchase_amt ord_date customer_id salesman_id
---------- ---------- ---------- ----------- --------- --
70001 150.5 2012-10-05 3005 5002
70009 270.65 2012-09-10 3001 5005
70002 65.26 2012-10-05 3002 5001
70004 110.5 2012-08-17 3009 5003
70007 948.5 2012-09-10 3005 5002
70005 2400.6 2012-07-27 3007 5001
70008 5760 2012-09-10 3002 5001
70010 1983.43 2012-10-10 3004 5006
70003 2480.4 2012-10-10 3009 5003
70012 250.45 2012-06-27 3008 5002
70011 75.29 2012-08-17 3003 5007
70013 3045.6 2012-04-25 3002 5001
```

Solution example:

```
SELECT ord_no, ord_date, purch_amt
FROM orders
WHERE salesman_id=5001;
```

Query output:

```
ord_no ord_date purchase_amt
70002 2012-10-05 65.26
70005 2012-07-27 2400.60
70008 2012-09-10 5760.00
70013 2012-04-25 3045.60
```

6. Write an SQL query to display the Nobel Prizes for 1970.

```
YEAR SUBJECT WINNER COUNTRY CATEGORY
---- ----------------------------------------------------- ----------

1970 Physics Hannes Alfven Sweden Scientist
1970 Physics Louis Neel France Scientist
1970 Chemistry Luis Federico Leloir France Scientist
1970 Physiology Ulf von Euler Sweden Scientist
1970 Physiology Bernard Katz Germany Scientist
1970 Literature Alexander Solzhenitsyn Russia Linguist
1970 Economics Paul Samuelson USA Economist
1970 Physiology Julius Axelrod USA Scientist
1971 Physics Dennis Gabor Hungary Scientist
1971 Chemistry Gerhard Herzberg Germany Scientist
1971 Peace Willy Brandt Germany Chancellor
1971 Literature Pablo Neruda Chile Linguist
1971 Economics Simon Kuznets Russia Economist
1978 Peace Anwar al-Sadat Egypt President
1978 Peace Menachem Begin Israel Prime Minister
1987 Chemistry Donald J. Cram USA Scientist
1987 Chemistry Jean-Marie Lehn France Scientist
1987 Physiology Susumu Tonegawa Japan Scientist
1994 Economics Reinhard Selten Germany Economist
1994 Peace Yitzhak Rabin Israel Prime Minister
1987 Physics Johannes Georg Bednorz Germany Scientist
1987 Literature Joseph Brodsky Russia Linguist
1987 Economics Robert Solow USA Economist
1994 Literature Kenzaburo Oe Japan Linguist
```

Solution example:

```
SELECT year,subject,winner
FROM nobel_win
WHERE year=1970;
```

Query output:

```
winner of the year
1970 Physics Hannes Alfven
1970 Physics Louis Neal
1970 Chemistry Luis Federico Leloir
1970 Physiology Julius Axelrod
1970 Physiology Ulf von Euler
1970 Physiology Bernard Katz
1970 Literature Alexander Solzhenitsyn
1970 Economics Paul Samuelson
```

7. Write an SQL query to determine the 1971 Literature Prize winner.

```
YEAR SUBJECT WINNER COUNTRY CATEGORY
---- -------- ------------------------------------- ----------

1970 Physics Hannes Alfven Sweden Scientist
1970 Physics Louis Neel France Scientist
1970 Chemistry Luis Federico Leloir France Scientist
1970 Physiology Ulf von Euler Sweden Scientist
1970 Physiology Bernard Katz Germany Scientist
1970 Literature Alexander Solzhenitsyn Russia Linguist
1970 Economics Paul Samuelson USA Economist
1970 Physiology Julius Axelrod USA Scientist
1971 Physics Dennis Gabor Hungary Scientist
1971 Chemistry Gerhard Herzberg Germany Scientist
1971 Peace Willy Brandt Germany Chancellor
1971 Literature Pablo Neruda Chile Linguist
1971 Economics Simon Kuznets Russia Economist
1978 Peace Anwar al-Sadat Egypt President
1978 Peace Menachem Begin Israel Prime Minister
1987 Chemistry Donald J. Cram USA Scientist
1987 Chemistry Jean-Marie Lehn France Scientist
1987 Physiology Susumu Tonegawa Japan Scientist
1994 Economics Reinhard Selten Germany Economist
1994 Peace Yitzhak Rabin Israel Prime Minister
1987 Physics Johannes Georg Bednorz Germany Scientist
1987 Literature Joseph Brodsky Russia Linguist
1987 Economics Robert Solow USA Economist
1994 Literature Kenzaburo Oe Japan Linguist
```

Solution example:

SELECT winner

 FROM nobel_win

WHERE year = 1971

 AND subject ='Literature';

Query output:

winner

Pablo Neruda

Chapter 3: Exercises Using Boolean and Relational Operators

1) Write a query statement to display all New York customers with a rating value greater than 100.

```
customer_id | custom_name | city | grade | salesman_id
-------------+-----------------+------------+------ -+-------------
    3002 | Nick Rimando | new york | 100 | 5001
    3007 | Brad Davis | new york | 200 | 5001
    3005 | Graham Zusi | California | 200 | 5002
    3008 | Julian Green | London | 300 | 5002
    3004 | Fabian Johnson | Paris | 300 | 5006
    3009 | Geoff Cameron | Berlin | 100 | 5003
    3003 | Jozy Altidor | Moscow | 200 | 5007
    3001 | Brad Guzan | London | | 5005
```

Solution example:

```
SELECT *
FROM customer
WHERE city ='New York' AND grade>100;
```

Query output:

```
customer_id cust_name city rating seller_id
3007 Brad Davis NY 200 5001
```

2) Write an SQL statement to display all customers that belong to New York City or have a score greater than 100.

```
customer_id | custom_name | city | grade | salesman_id
-------------+-------------------+-------------+------ -+----
        3002 | Nick Rimando | new york | 100 | 5001
        3007 | Brad Davis | new york | 200 | 5001
        3005 | Graham Zusi | California | 200 | 5002
        3008 | Julian Green | London | 300 | 5002
        3004 | Fabian Johnson | Paris | 300 | 5006
        3009 | Geoff Cameron | Berlin | 100 | 5003
        3003 | Jozy Altidor | Moscow | 200 | 5007
        3001 | Brad Guzan | London | | 5005
```

Solution example:

```
SELECT *
FROM customer
WHERE city ='New York' OR grade>100;
```

Query output:

```
customer_id cust_name city rating seller_id
3002 Nick Rimando New York 100 5001
3007 Brad Davis NY 200 5001
3005 Graham Zusi California 200 5002
3008 Julian Green London 300 5002
3004 Fabian Johnson Paris 300 5006
3003 Josi Altidore Moscow 200 5007
```

3) Write a SQL query to find data about employees whose last name is Dosney or Mardy.

```
EMP_IDNO EMP_FNAME EMP_LNAME EMP_DEPT
--------- -------------- -------------------------
   127323 Michale Robbin 57
   526689 Carlos Snares 63
   843795 Enric Dosio 57
   328717 Jhon Snares 63
   444527 Joseph Dosni 47
   659831 Zanifer Emily 47
   847674 Kuleswar Sitaraman 57
   748681 Henrey Gabriel 47
   555935 Alex Manuel 57
   539569 George Mardy 27
   733843 Mario Saule 63
   631548 Alan Snappy 27
   839139 Maria Foster 57
```

Solution example:

```
SELECT *
 FROM emp_details
  WHERE emp_lname ='Dosni' OR emp_lname='Mardy';
```

Query output:

```
emp_idno emp_fname emp_lname emp_dept
444527 Joseph Dosney 47
539569 George Mardi 27
```

4) Write a query in SQL to display all data of employees who work in departments 47 or 63.

```
EMP_IDNO EMP_FNAME EMP_LNAME EMP_DEPT
--------- --------------- -------------------------
    127323 Michale Robbin 57
    526689 Carlos Snares 63
    843795 Enric Dosio 57
    328717 Jhon Snares 63
    444527 Joseph Dosni 47
    659831 Zanifer Emily 47
    847674 Kuleswar Sitaraman 57
    748681 Henrey Gabriel 47
    555935 Alex Manuel 57
    539569 George Mardy 27
    733843 Mario Saule 63
    631548 Alan Snappy 27
    839139 Maria Foster 57
```

Solution example:

```
SELECT *
 FROM emp_details
  WHERE emp_dept = 47 OR emp_dept = 63;
```

Query output:

```
emp_idno emp_fname emp_lname emp_dept
526689 Carlos Snares 63
328717 Jhon Snares 63
444527 Joseph Dosney 47
659831 Zanifer Emily 47
748681 Henry Gabriel 47
733843 Mario Saule 63
```

5) Write an SQL query to display the order number, purchase amount, and achieved and unreached percentage (%) for those orders that exceed 50% of the target value of 6000.

ord_no purchase_amt ord_date customer_id salesman_id
---------- ---------- ---------- ----------- --------- --
70001 150.5 2012-10-05 3005 5002
70009 270.65 2012-09-10 3001 5005
70002 65.26 2012-10-05 3002 5001
70004 110.5 2012-08-17 3009 5003
70007 948.5 2012-09-10 3005 5002
70005 2400.6 2012-07-27 3007 5001
70008 5760 2012-09-10 3002 5001
70010 1983.43 2012-10-10 3004 5006
70003 2480.4 2012-10-10 3009 5003
70012 250.45 2012-06-27 3008 5002
70011 75.29 2012-08-17 3003 5007
70013 3045.6 2012-04-25 3002 5001

Solution example:

```
SELECT ord_no,purch_amt,
(100*purch_amt)/6000 AS "Achieved %",
(100*(6000-purch_amt)/6000) AS "Unachieved %"
FROM orders
WHERE (100*purch_amt)/6000>50;
```

Query output:

ord_no purchase_amt Completed % Not completed %
70008 5760.00 96.0000000000000000 4.0000000000000000
70013 3045.60 50.7600000000000000 49.2400000000000000

6) Write an SQL statement to exclude rows that satisfy the following:
- the order date is 2012-08-17, and the purchase amount is less than 1000
- the customer ID is greater than 3005, and the purchase amount is less than 1000.

ord_no purchase_amt ord_date customer_id salesman_id
---------- ---------- ---------- ----------- --------- --
70001 150.5 2012-10-05 3005 5002
70009 270.65 2012-09-10 3001 5005
70002 65.26 2012-10-05 3002 5001
70004 110.5 2012-08-17 3009 5003
70007 948.5 2012-09-10 3005 5002
70005 2400.6 2012-07-27 3007 5001
70008 5760 2012-09-10 3002 5001
70010 1983.43 2012-10-10 3004 5006
70003 2480.4 2012-10-10 3009 5003
70012 250.45 2012-06-27 3008 5002
70011 75.29 2012-08-17 3003 5007
70013 3045.6 2012-04-25 3002 5001

Solution example:

```
SELECT *
FROM orders
WHERE NOT((ord_date ='2012-08-17'
OR customer_id>3005)
AND purch_amt<1000);
```

Query output:

ord_no purchase_amt ord_date customer_id salesman_id
70009 270.65 2012-09-10 3001 5005
70002 65.26 2012-10-05 3002 5001
70005 2400.60 2012-07-27 3007 5001
70008 5760.00 2012-09-10 3002 5001
70010 1983.43 2012-10-10 3004 5006
70003 2480.40 2012-10-10 3009 5003
70013 3045.60 2012-04-25 3002 5001
70001 150.50 2012-10-05 3005 5002
70007 948.50 2012-09-10 3005 5002

7) Write an SQL query to display all orders for which the purchase amount is less than 200 or to exclude those orders whose order date is at least February 10, 2012, and the customer ID is less than 3009.

ord_no purchase_amt ord_date customer_id salesman_id
---------- ---------- ---------- ---------- --------- --
70001 150.5 2012-10-05 3005 5002
70009 270.65 2012-09-10 3001 5005
70002 65.26 2012-10-05 3002 5001
70004 110.5 2012-08-17 3009 5003
70007 948.5 2012-09-10 3005 5002
70005 2400.6 2012-07-27 3007 5001
70008 5760 2012-09-10 3002 5001
70010 1983.43 2012-10-10 3004 5006
70003 2480.4 2012-10-10 3009 5003
70012 250.45 2012-06-27 3008 5002
70011 75.29 2012-08-17 3003 5007
70013 3045.6 2012-04-25 3002 5001

Solution example:

```
SELECT *
FROM orders
WHERE(purch_amt<200 OR
NOT(ord_date>='2012-02-10'
AND customer_id<3009));
```

Query output:

ord_no purchase_amt ord_date customer_id salesman_id
70002 65.26 2012-10-05 3002 5001
70004 110.50 2012-08-17 3009 5003
70003 2480.40 2012-10-10 3009 5003
70011 75.29 2012-08-17 3003 5007
70001 150.50 2012-10-05 3005 5002

References

https://www.w3schools.com/sql/sql_intro.asp

https://sqlbolt.com/

https://www.datacamp.com/courses/introduction-to-sqlhttps://sqlzoo.net/wiki/SQL_Tutorial

https://online.stanford.edu/courses/soe-ydatabases0005-databases-relational-databases-and-sql

https://www.techtarget.com/searchdatamanagement/definition/SQL

SQL COOKBOOK query solutions and techniques for all sql users by ANTHONY MOLINARO

https://www.spiceworks.com/tech/artificial-intelligence/articles/what-is-sql/

https://www.javatpoint.com/mysql-tutorial

https://www.w3schools.com/mysql/mysql_sql.asp

https://www.javatpoint.com/dbms-sql-command

https://beginnersbook.com/2022/07/dbms-sql-commands-ddl-dml-dcl-tcl-and-dql/#:~:text=DDL%20(Data%20Definition%20Language)%20%E2%80%93,Commands%20such%20as%20COMMIT%2C%20ROLLBACK.

https://www.geeksforgeeks.org/sql

https://codewithmosh.com/courses/525068/lectures/9590156

https://grownwith.us/mysql-tutorial-for-beginners/471/1

https://learn.microsoft.com/en-us/sql/relational-databases/performance/joins

https://www.postgresqltutorial.com/

https://databear.com/data-preparation-part-2-pivot-vs-unpivot-columns/

https://stackoverflow.com/questions/21893462/sequential-sql-inserts-when-triggered-by-cross-apply

https://www.stratascratch.com/blog/sql-interview-questions-you-must-prepare-the-ultimate-guide/

Learning SQL Master SQL Fundamentals by Alan Beaulieu

Head First SQL by Lynn Beighley

SQL For Dummies Allen G. Taylor

Made in the USA
Monee, IL
16 February 2023

27954079R10090